D0360051

My Grandfather's Book

Books by Gary Gildner

POETRY

The Bunker in the Parsley Fields 1997
Clackamas 1991
Blue Like the Heavens: New & Selected Poems 1984
The Runner 1978
Nails 1975
Digging for Indians 1971
First Practice 1969

LIMITED EDITIONS

The Birthday Party 2000
The Swing 1996
Pavol Hudák, the Poet, Is Talking 1996
Jabón 1981
Letters from Vicksburg 1976
Eight Poems 1973

FICTION

The Second Bridge 1987
A Week in South Dakota 1987
The Crush 1983

MEMOIR

The Warsaw Sparks 1990
My Grandfather's Book: Generations of an American Family 2002

ANTHOLOGY

Out of This World: Poems from the Hawkeye State 1975

My Grandfather's Book

Generations of an American Family

GARY GILDNER

Michigan State University Press
East Lansing

∞ The paper used in this publication meets the minimum requirements of ANSI/NISO Z39.48–1992 (R 1997) (Permanence of Paper).
Michigan State University Press
East Lansing, Michigan 48823-5245

Printed and bound in the United States of America.
08 07 06 05 04 03 02 1 2 3 4 5 6 7 8 9 10

LIBRARY OF CONGRESS CATALOGING-IN-PUBLICATION DATA

Gildner, Gary.
My grandfather's book : generations of an American family / Gary Gildner.
p. cm.
ISBN 0-87013-639-9 (alk. paper)
1. Gildner, Gary—Family. 2. Gildner, Gary—Childhood and youth. 3. Authors, American—20th century—Family relationships. 4. Authors, American—20th century—Bibliography. 5. Grandparent and child—United States. 6. Polish Americans—Bibliography. 7. Family—United States. I. Title.
PS3557.I343 Z468
811'.54—dc21
2002004603

Cover design by Sans Serif Inc., Saline, Michigan
Book design by Sans Serif Inc., Saline, Michigan

Visit Michigan State University Press on the World Wide Web at:
www.msupress.msu.edu

Acknowledgments

I am grateful to the editors of the following publications in whose pages certain chapters of this book first appeared—in some cases in different form: "In the Presence of the Clearwater," *The Georgia Review;* "Documents," *Great River Review;* "Beginning My Education," *Horse People;* "Recalling the Last Day," *The North American Review;* "Early Spring: The Cougar" and "Covering Ground," *New Letters;* "Keys," "Alphabets and Maps," "Expression," "A Kind of Fable," and "Where To?" *The Southern Review;* "Introduction to the Trail," *Witness.* Brief selections of the book also appeared in *Artful Dodge, Clockwatch Review, Field, Forkroads, Poetry Northwest,* and *River Oak Review.* "A Song" and my short story "Sleepy Time Gal," which Stan Lindberg first published in *The Georgia Review,* have much in common.

The past is a foreign country:
they do things differently there.

—L.P. Hartley

We are all immigrants.

—Anon.

Only true love can save me.

—Margaret, at 5, eyes closed, lying in her tub

Contents

Introduction to the Trail 1
Keys 11
Alphabets and Maps 20
Documents 27
Expression 46
A Kind of Fable 58
Recalling the Last Day 64
Where To? 82
Bringing Home the Baby 91
Early Spring: The Cougar 97
In the Presence of the Clearwater 103
Beginning My Education 110
Just a Boy 116
A Song 124
Where Am I? 131
Work Hard and Die 139
A Snapshot 152
The River 163
Hail Columbia 173
The Old Country and the New 187
Great Odds 198
A Flock of Small Birds 210
A Stupendous Grave 219
At Least One Pure Disappearing Act 232
Covering Ground 239

Introduction to the Trail

We live on a mountain. The sun comes up over Blacktail Ridge across the valley, crosses the Clearwater River, and lights up the fruit trees I planted, the garden, the barn, the corral, and of course this house, which is full of windows. The window in the room where I work faces The Gospels an hour away. I note the snow on their peaks, the clouds that rub them into another season. The large window in Lizzie's studio, directly behind her drawing table, had two fawns beside it this morning, watching her. Not too many mornings ago, it seems, the cougar that prowls our mountain came down to the corral just as Lizzie was nursing Margaret in the rocking chair in front of Margaret's window. "Look out the back door," I heard her call.

Even the barn has windows. Big picture windows. The cat that adopted us sits on a bar stool Lizzie put behind one of the windows so it can watch the bats at night. She named it Yah teh, "hello" in Navajo.

We bought this place a year before we actually moved in. We bought it because my visiting appointment in North Carolina was ending and we really didn't want to return to Iowa, where our legal residence and our permanent jobs were, and because the Fulbright to Hungary I had been nominated for had fallen through. We also bought it because out of the North Carolina blue one day Lizzie said, "I've never been to Idaho, but I think I'd like to live there." I had been there, years before, and off and on had had the same thought.

So we drove to Idaho. I had friends in the Clearwater Valley who would help us. Wayne worked for Fish and Game, Randy taught high school English; they owned forty acres and a raft. We gave ourselves two weeks to see how we felt out there, what kind of house we might find.

Were we honestly thinking to *move?* asked my in-laws, who lived in Des Moines. Did either of us have a job out there? They didn't understand what our plan was. I was a tenured professor at Drake and Lizzie, having eased away from *Better Homes and Gardens,* had her own graphics business. She made the mistake of using words such as "retire," "write," and "art" in trying to explain.

Her father latched on to the one he knew best. "Retire?" he said. He himself had retired from his job at seventy-two. Reluctantly. I had twenty years to go before reaching that mark, his daughter more than thirty.

What she meant, she said, was something else. But no good words would come to her.

"Retire?" he said, as if this one were nasty.

Like the story goes, we found our spot, our mountain retreat, on the last day. We wanted it. That same day I got a call from the Fulbright office in Washington (tracked down via my in-laws, who had Wayne and Randy's phone number). An appointment was suddenly available in Czechoslovakia. Was I interested? I was. It would give me a chance to see, up close, how the story was turning out over there. It would also take me back very close to the area, in southern Poland, where my maternal grandfather, Stefan Szostak, had been born. In 1987 and 1988, when I lived in Warsaw, I didn't know the name of his village, and even if I had known I probably would not have tried to find it, caught up as I was in the story I tell in *The Warsaw Sparks,* about coaching a Polish baseball team. When I returned to the States and started to write my grandfather's story—or the story of my search for him—I learned that his birthplace was called Ostrów. It was just north of the Tatra Mountains.

Now I could go look. I asked Lizzie what she thought. She said yes. So we bought the Idaho place, finally, because we wanted to come back here: because the man selling it to us, Joe, had been an art major in college and had built the house as he went along, as he would paint a picture, changing whole areas according to the light; and the light he caught was the kind we wanted to end up in.

We drove to Des Moines to pack. My in-laws were relieved, I think, that at least one of us had a job now, even if it was in a country that was planning to break in half.

In Czechoslovakia, before and after it broke up that year, we lived in a State-designed flat, a cement box an hour downwind from the Tatras. But we couldn't see them, surrounded as we were by hundreds of other flats exactly like ours. We could look out our sixth-floor window, straight down, and see the abandoned bunker, and at a certain hour watch a small boy bang his trike, over and over, against the bunker's thick wall. I was there, officially, to teach American literature. Free-wheeling Whitman ranked high with my students, stay-at-home Thoreau low, but no matter whom we read they didn't want too much. We didn't need to read *all* of "Song of Myself," for example; three or four lines, to get the general idea, was enough, one of my students announced. Vlado was a member of the last class to enter the university under the old system, the system recently thrown out by the Velvet Revolution, and he was in a hurry to "get going." Where are you going? I asked him. After thinking it over, he shrugged and said, "Everywhere." Vlado was a prize-winning young poet, and included in that "everywhere" was his plan to get a good teaching job.

We were brothers, of a kind. I was a teacher and a writer, and I had had those two jobs for a long time—in at least five states and two or three foreign countries. And before I became a teacher and a writer I was a hack who wanted not to be a hack, and before that I was a college student working summers in an ice cream factory, winters delivering Christmas mail, and before that I was a high school jock digging bomb shelters (briefly) for a Minister of God—or so he said—and before that I caddied golf clubs, owned a newspaper route, mowed lawns, helped my dad.

"What does dad do?" I once asked my mother. I was filling out a school form that had a space for Father's Occupation. "Put down Home Improvement," she said.

Two key questions when I was growing up: Where do you live and what does your dad do? In my eyes he did a lot of different things. He fixed the car, the leaky faucet, the furnace, my wagon, the nail in my boot, my mother's mixer, the toaster. To an aching molar one time he tied a gut leader, the leader to his hammer, and swung, fixing his own tooth. A dentist would have taken longer, gummed up his whole day, and made him pay besides. This way he was wide awake, right back to work, and

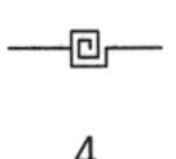

nothing hurt. He was a member of that generation of men who were their own experts and wore a hat when they dressed up, curling the brim just so; who, driving from here to there, "made good time," or resting an arm in the open window, went for "a spin." He could take apart the engine of his 1936 Chevrolet coupe—down to the last gasket—and put it all back. He could grow perfect tomatoes, make beer, nap after lunch on a stack of two-by-fours in the shade, shave his whiskers, after letting them go a day, as if there were no greater pleasure. But what he *did,* officially, was Home Improvement.

"Why not say carpenter?"

"You could say that. But the other sounds nicer."

My mother was right, I now think. He did improve the home. Although what she meant was something else. That something else, I figure, is connected to romance. My mother has always been fond of—crazy for, she has said—the movies. She once told me she must have been named for Jean Harlow. (Jean Harlow, the actress, was five when Jean Szostak was born.) She has also said that my sister and I were named for Gloria Swanson and Gary Cooper, though my brother, she says, was named for Gregory Peck *and* a pope. "Which one?" "The tall one!" Recalling the time of her courtship when my dad came calling on his Indian motorcycle, she has closed her eyes and said, "I'll tell you *exactly* who your dad looked like then. Alan Ladd."

When I was a hack for Fred Waring, working out of his posh resort in the Poconos, my parents came to visit me. Although Waring—of Fred Waring and the Pennsylvanians—was not exactly my mother's idea of a movie star, he *had* been in the movies, and was handsome enough, and his Shawnee-on-Delaware Inn was glamorous. Moreover, on the day I showed her and my father around the premises, Jackie Gleason and Howard Keel were right over there, about to tee off, and I, her son, was among them, in my Stanley Blacker lime green blazer, working. Seeing my office, my apartment, my convertible parked in my own space, she sighed. "My god, you're lucky. What a job." What I did was write "features" about the place, "color pieces." The idea was to get ink in the papers.

My immediate boss was an old radio buddy of Fred's named Harry. Eight-by-ten glossy photos of Harry hung almost everywhere on his walls. Harry behind a mike with Crosby, with Jack Benny. Harry arm-in-arm with Dempsey, with Toots Shor. All of the photos were autographed to a great guy, a pal, one in a million. He looked over my copy and always praised it and, handing it back, always said, "But maybe a little more schmaltz, kid, huh? People go for schmaltz, believe me." Harry wore a big bow tie and a big smile, just like in the pictures on his walls, and when, after three months, I told him I was leaving, he smiled and said, "Kid, I hope you know what you're doing."

The first meaning in exactly four inches of definition of *do* in my dictionary says: "To perform, as an action; fabricate or compose, as a piece of work." This makes me smile—for lots of reasons. Once a man who owned a big well-drilling outfit said to me, "I hear you're a writer." I nodded. "I write a little myself," he said. "What kind of computer do you use?" Some years ago a poet wanted to show me what she'd done with her Guggenheim money. I followed her upstairs. "This used to be the guest room," she said. "It was perfect." Perfect, she meant, to accommodate all the computer and printing machinery she'd purchased. Among other things she no longer had to do, she said, was retype an entire poem if a word needed changing. The dean of my college once said to me, concerned, "You are the only member of the entire faculty who has refused a free Apple for his office."

I write, I work, I *do* with a pencil; while he was alive, it was the one tool I had in common with my father. He carried his over his ear, the point tucked under his cap. At the end of the day his gray sideburn was lead-black. For myself I like how the words come out of my head and travel down my arm to that sharp point. I like holding a pencil. Also a baseball, a smooth stone fresh from the river, a walking stick, my daughter's hand.

To perform, as an action; fabricate or compose. . . . When I left the Poconos I went directly back to East Lansing, for an M.A., for a degree that could help me get a college teaching job, since I did need a job to support my habit of doing, or trying to do, stories like those I admired—Hemingway's, Fitzgerald's, Babel's, Conrad's. Mrs. Brown, the classic, if not classical, little old lady on my draft board, was delighted, when I appeared before her, to be able to appoint the holder of an M.A. proctor of the bus taking the boys down to Fort Sill. I could not find the best words in the best order to tell her that the holder of an M.A. in comparative literature was not the best person for the job.

Joseph Conrad, I discovered almost at the last minute, was Stefan Szostak's favorite writer. I did not know this when, as a boy, I followed him around his Michigan farm. My parents sent me "up north" those summers—from Flint—to learn a few things. I learned that Grandpa sometimes sat in his orchard—in the middle of the work day—and looked at the sky. For hours, it seemed. I knew something about farmers from my dad's side of the family and *they* didn't do that. When taking his big Belgians down to the creek for a drink, he'd go in with them, boots and all, and lay his face on the water, his mustache spread out like fine muzzle hairs, sun-struck drops clinging to it when he rose up, shaking like the horses, satisfied. Once he pulled me up to the hay wagon, sat me between his knees and put the reins in my hands. Helping me steer we raced up and down the field—*gee!* and *haw!*—and when Grandma came rushing out, her fists, her skirts, and the Polish flying, afraid I would be hurt, he helped me turn the wagon around and around her. Nights after chores, in the kerosene lamp's honeyed glow, he ate his soup and bread, knelt beside the chair and said his rosary, then poured a glass of whiskey and opened a book. Night after night. I remember that, and that he seemed, reading, to disappear.

The summer I stayed in Flint to start baseball, they found him beside the orchard. On my eleventh birthday, in a satin-lined box, he lay with pennies on his eyes, his trimmed mustache an almost perfect caterpillar. Just before Mr. Savage the undertaker closed the coffin, Grandma put in there the last book he was reading, the one they had found him with. I did not see this. Years later, on my way to Iowa to start a new teaching job, Grandma told me—reminded of it, she said, by all the books in my car. I wanted very much to know the name of that book. She couldn't tell me. Only that it was by "this Korzeniowski again, always Korzeniowski," she said.

Over drinks at a poetry festival, where I was to introduce him, I was telling Czeslaw Milosz about my grandfather. "I think that last book was *Heart of Darkness.*" He raised his eyebrows, raised his glass. Was there a better title to take into eternity?

On the spring day when Lizzie and I arrived in Ostrów, a stork lifted off from its nest on a pole across from the village cemetery and flew directly over us. I do not intend a pun in that last sentence; a pole supported the nest, there is no other word for it. Moreover, she was pregnant.

We had no way of knowing when we bought our Idaho place that what would make it complete for us was a child, nor that we had to go to Czechoslovakia for her, specifically to the Tatra Mountains, which are a lot like the mountains around here. The day Lizzie gave me the news we were walking beside the Danube. She was almost forty; she had almost "given up the idea." I had just bought some apples and plums. The first thing I did when we got home was plant an orchard of apples and plums.

Certain phrases stick. A dentist once told me, "Pain moves around." Boys I played baseball with, who stayed in Flint and got jobs in the factories—"at good pay"—years later were "putting their time in." They called themselves "shop rats." My best buddy, Eddie Hill, who taught me how to throw a roundhouse curve, how to drop-kick a football, how to pole vault, and how to scale a perch with beer caps nailed on a stick, used to exclaim, when he was surprised at something, "Well, shake the dew!" The complete expression went, "Well, shake the dew off my lily!" To gloss this language would coarsen it, delete from the poetry. Eddie died of heart failure the year my daughter turned two, the year she started to say, "I can do this!"

Probably the one member of my family who would understand what I do was the one I never exchanged a single word with. He was splashed by molten steel in Henry Ford's foundry, my mother said, then left Detroit, retired, and became a farmer. He made this move in a fabulous year, 1927, when Babe Ruth hit sixty home runs, Charles Augustus ("Lucky") Lindbergh soloed the Atlantic, and the stock market was soaring. He became a farmer and read Joseph Conrad translated into Polish, the only language he ever spoke.

When he was alive my father never asked what I did, because it was obvious: I was a professor. It was also obvious (and a little glamorous) to my mother. But now that I have quit "that line of work" she wonders. So does my sister, who was valedictorian of her high school class. Out to see us last summer, Gloria asked me, "What do you *do* all day?"

"Well, in the mornings I write."

"Well, I know *that,*" she said. "I mean in all this space!"

Space—distance—all of the in between here and there—is hard to talk about. So is how we earn our living. What we *can* say is that we like to "put in a good day's work." We don't really like "working for the other guy." Although working for the other guy has its advantages, we would prefer, given the opportunity, "working for ourselves." Given the opportunity.

My brother prefers sailing his boat on the Great Lakes to "pounding nails." He once built a house, sold it, and realized later he forgot to include the cost of the land. He laughs about this, graving his hull. My mother—who is still fond of movies—wonders "what will happen to the poor guy." She knows what will happen. We all know what will happen. And if we're lucky it will happen when we are dreaming.

Every day now on waking I walk down the mountain exactly a mile, over the old trail tramped by a man and his mule, a miner I'm told, some dreamer who failed, going round and round, the snow letting go, giving way to burnt gold grasses and brown stones unbending, rolling, the perfect tracks all slipping their grips, all losing themselves in the new wash, this walk we share and share again, a rhythm, a race, almost a religion with no book, no one to lay on the laurel, the meaning, no loud exclamations, a quiet step followed by another, a whistle, a bird, a little flick of light let loose and falling among the gravel.

Keys

In Prague, when Lizzie and I asked a Czech official about taking the train to Prešov, she said, "I do not advise the train. It is a filthy method. The only way to Slovakia, if one must go there, is by plane." She made a face like someone who had just lost a filling.

I exchanged money—dollars for crowns. On the 100 crown note a man and woman stood side by side, he wearing welder's gear, his shirt open exposing his chest, she in overalls, a babushka, a sheaf of wheat under her arm. In the background, tall industrial chimneys poured smoke into the sky. The couple gazed straight ahead, a pair of workers sharing the load. They

might have been drawn by Norman Rockwell, except there was no humor, no irony, no surprises in their faces or anywhere else . . . unless you counted a kind of halo constructed out of a gear wheel, wheat berries, and coils of steel that hovered over their heads. Once upon a time they were the new saints, but who knew what they were now: this bank note was pre-revolution (pre-1989) and would soon be replaced.

We bought train tickets to Prešov, which lay ten hours to the east, almost in Ukraine. Our compartment was clean and comfortable, and what we saw out the window we could not have seen from a plane: kids beating dust from rugs, a flock of geese following an old woman single-file across a field, tidy apple orchards whose cidery scent wafted our way. In the small towns we passed through, the stationmasters stood at attention in their doorways, hats on, shoulders back, and saluted us. We went between autumn hills, through tunnels into piney corridors, past streams, beside a lake that reflected our waving arms. I was fifty-four, Lizzie thirty-eight—the one and only time, she pointed out, in which my age would match the year of her birth and her age would match the year of mine. I thought about chance and how I was now a grandfather traveling to Slovakia and would have a chance to walk in the Polish village that my grandfather, then a teenager, had walked away from, carrying his loaf of bread. I thought about a novel called *Chance* by Joseph Conrad and wondered if that was the book in my grandfather's coffin. It was a good title to take into eternity, though *Heart of Darkness* was better. I thought about how intently he gazed into the northern Michigan sky those summers he sat in his apple orchard while I, a boy in a tree, watched him and wondered, as I wondered on the train, what he was looking for.

Outside Prešov we were delivered to a huge housing estate called Sečov, named for a little brook that the estate's development had destroyed. We learned this later. We also learned that our street in Sečov—Dumbierska—meant something like "ginger," that the road connecting us to downtown Prešov was called Sibirska—meaning Siberia—and that the number 38 bus would carry us back and forth on Sibirska for two crowns. But the first time we went to Sečov it was in Igor's Skoda, at night, and he was laughing and saying he was trying not to get lost.

After the lush, dreamy countryside we'd been looking at all day, ending up here was sobering. The pre-fab high-rises surrounded us. I tried to count them once—weeks later—and lost interest. They all looked alike—cement-colored, nine stories—dormitories plunked down in a raw, treeless setting. The one we stopped at was new, Igor told us. "You will be the first occupants of your flat!"

An elevator not much larger than a telephone booth—basically a platform in a shaft—took us up six floors. You could touch the building's skeleton as you rose. Igor, squeezed in with us, said in his acquired British accent, "Is it all right then?" He'd said the same thing pointing at our mailbox down in the entryway. He was my chairman at the university, a man who got up on the balls of his feet a lot and showed you the big gap between his two front teeth, his eyes bulging. He had met our train and brought us directly to "the new digs," as he called them, where he commenced to show us all our keys: building key, mailbox key, flat key, and the remaining six that—he demonstrated—would unlock the bedroom, living room, toilet, bathroom, kitchen, and a large foyer closet.

"Is it all right then?"

"Yes, well, everything looks fine." I didn't know what else to say. The important business seemed to be that all the keys worked.

"Fine then." He shook our hands. "Cheerio." He started to leave, and stopped. "Oh, did you bring food?"

"Food?"

"You're not hungry, I hope."

We said we were fine.

"Fine then. Ah yes, Professor Grmela and his wife will call on you tomorrow with certain details. Cheerio."

Igor and the man who had brought up our luggage disappeared down the elevator. Lizzie and I stood in our foyer and looked at the metal doors surrounding us, then at each other and laughed. So here we were, in Slovakia, on a Saturday night in September, with a string of nine keys.

A TV sat in the living room. We turned it on. A beauty contest was in progress. Young women paraded in evening gowns, in bathing suits. They all had long gorgeous legs and exaggerated the swing in their hips as if parodying beauty contestants. They took turns caressing a new Skoda, falling into new sofas, having their high shiny cheekbones dusted with powders, modeling fur coats and leather motorcycle jackets and jewelry; they held up glossy photos of cocktail lounges and swimming pools and airplanes in which people about to take a drink or dive or fly away waved to us. All of these products and pictures were praised by a tux-tucked, toothy master of ceremonies. When he paused, a voice off-camera sang, in English, "Only you can make my life complete." Almost every Saturday night, we discovered, we could turn on the TV and see a beauty contest like this one.

In the middle of the night we were wakened by a wail that might have been an outburst of grief or an attempt at song. Or both. It came from the flat above us. It was a man's voice, and if he was in pain his long, melancholy cry seemed to say that no one, no one could help him. But then we heard a woman's voice—from the same place—and its bark-like syllables apparently came to his rescue. In a few moments the man's wail trailed off into silence. This, too, seemed a regular weekend event.

Looking out our living room window, straight down, we could see what appeared to be a gigantic unfinished basement. It seemed as long and wide as a soccer field, had partitions for rooms, and was full of water. This, we would learn, had been the start of a neighborhood bunker; work on it, however, came to an immediate halt the day the revolution arrived because the men and women building it no longer knew who would pay them for their labor and walked off the job. There it sat, three years now, collecting rain, tossed stones, tossed refuse, and rats.

Almost daily the small boy would appear on his tricycle and ram into the bunker's outer wall. After ramming it, he would back up a few yards, lower his head and, pedaling hard, ram into the wall again. He did this over and over. At first we feared he would become bored with not getting anywhere and climb on the wall—which was not much taller than he was—to see what he might do up there, and maybe fall into the water. But he never got off his trike that we could see; he had a mission, a job, somewhere to get to—and this thing, this stupidity, was in his path. It made him mad, and ramming it was all he could do, until his mother arrived to lead him away.

That first Sunday morning, Anita and Nicole, the daughters of Josef and Anna Grmela, arrived at our door with bread, fruit, tea. "Our parents wish to come at noon and take you to lunch," said one. "They would have called, but you haven't a phone," said the other. Anita and Nicole were eighteen and seventeen, red-haired, freckled, cheerful, and curious.

"Are you glad you're here? I mean in Slovakia?" Nicole asked.

"Yes, we are," Lizzie said. "Aren't we, Doctor G.?"

"You call your husband by his title?" said Anita.

"It's a joke between us," Lizzie said. "I call him that, sometimes, because he's not a doctor."

"I know. American humor," Anita laughed.

"Weren't you a little afraid to come?" Nicole asked.

"What should we be afraid of?" Lizzie said.

"People here are afraid," Anita said. "They don't know what is going to happen after the separation."

"Even our parents are concerned," Nicole said.

"We're Czech, not Slovak," Anita said.

I asked where they lived. They took us to the living room window and pointed toward a small mountain in the distance.

"Šariš Castle is up there, or what remains."

"It resembled a cake."

"In fact eggs were used in the mortar."

"We will show you one day."

"And you live up there, on that mountain?" Lizzie said.

"No, no," Anita laughed. "Below it. In Development Number Three."

"But there is no egg in the mortar," Nicole said.

"No, it is not a cake, I'm afraid," Anita said.

The sisters left and their parents arrived, Anna vivacious as her daughters, Josef barrel-chested, red-bearded, freckled. They took us on the 38 bus to a hotel in town.

Anna said, "I know in the West, especially in America, I think, that people invite you in, not out. Here, strangely, it seems to be the reverse. But very soon, when things are calmer, you must come to our home." She consulted the menu. "Veal is their best dish. Is that all right?"

Josef said, "I for my part must avoid anything with flavor these days." He ordered carrots and soy croutons, and though he wanted coffee to drink, Anna said, "Not today, Josef."

"I never contradict my wife," he said. "It's the only rule I faithfully keep."

"He is having an experience," she said.

"Yes, for fifty years my kidneys enjoyed themselves and their work and never once complained. Now one of them, according to science, may be proposing a revolution. Very dull politics, believe me."

We liked the Grmelas. Words—conversation—seemed to make them spontaneously happy. Especially out in the open. If they had pointed to a leafy branch where we all might sit a while and imitate bird calls, I would not have been surprised. In the halls of the university, later, they would sound more like their colleagues, who did not sing, certainly not foolishly in a tree in the year when Czechoslovakia was splitting apart and everything, at any moment, might topple over. But on our first day with them, strolling cobbled streets almost 900 years old, there was nothing more dangerous around us than the subtle perfumes of autumn, a Gothic church, the Renaissance town hall, arches embedded with the heads of lions, faces with bulging eyes, and look, up there, on that chimney—a stork nest!

"Your Western imagination may be tickled to know that this historical center is called a reservation," Josef said.

At a sweet shop we bought ice cream cones—*zmrzlina*—and Lizzie pushed out her lips to try the word.

"*Shmers*lina!"

"Do you like it as well as American ice cream?" Anna asked her.

"Mmmm, maybe better. And I *think* it's my first cone since our wedding."

"Since your wedding!" Anna said

"We've only been married little more than a year," Lizzie told her.

"You're practically on your honeymoon then. Did you hear that, Josef? We should have a party!"

"If you will pardon me, I think honeymoons should be left entirely to the principals involved." He said this while keeping a careful eye on the single small dip of vanilla he'd been allowed.

Anna said, "I meant of course a party to honor their anniversary. In my excitement I wasn't clear."

"Perhaps," Josef said, "anniversaries early in a marriage are an even more delicate matter."

"He always talks like this," Anna said to us.

"Oh, not always."

"I mean when you are having fun, dear Josef."

"I am now reminded of my duty as a representative of the Philosophical Faculty to explain to our visiting Fulbright professor certain nuances, shall we say, in the academic system here."

"Please, Josef, we are enjoying our ice cream."

"The discussion about the quality of this food, in fact, reminded me of our grading methodology. Are you curious?" he asked me.

"Shoot."

"Yes, shoot. We have three grades—Excellent, Very good, and Good."

"No Fail?"

"If a student does not receive one of our three grades, he fails."

"So there are four grades."

"You could say so, but we count only the first three."

"Good must be the average grade, what we call C in the States."

"No. The most popular grade is Excellent, followed by Very Good. Almost no one receives Good, which is a disgraceful mark."

"Most of the students are above average?"

"Most are quite average. What I explained is what is done."

"Oh, Josef," Anna said, "look at the sky."

He did.

"Is it excellent?"

"Clearly."

"Is it complete and independent and pure, would you say?"

"I would say so."

"And beautiful?"

"That too, absolutely."

"Thank you."

Alphabets and Maps

The fall wind blew down all night from the Tatra Mountains, and sometimes we woke before dawn smelling the pine trees the wind had come through and told each other our dreams.

"I was studying Polish. Trying to carry the alphabet home across a field. I kept dropping letters in the tall grass."

"I was a girl again in Fort Madison, walking along the Mississippi searching for a little boat I had lost."

Once, after a dream about my grandfather, I looked at the Polish map. His village, Ostrów, by bus, would be roundabout, and that was all right, but we needed time. We didn't want to rush, and we wanted to be there in good weather. I also wanted to be ready, I told Lizzie, not exactly sure what I meant.

Often, those mornings, we went up the street to buy a round loaf of bread from the old woman who had baked it only hours before. I spoke broken Polish to her and she replied in Polish, laughing. She was always pleased that we preferred her specialty, the rye made with potatoes. Most mornings after breakfast I stayed in the flat to write and Lizzie took the 38 bus to my office. My office had excellent natural light from a large window facing north and was quiet, not near any other offices, and she could make her pastels, with the radio on, and not disturb anyone. She could also play the piano. The piano was in there, Josef suspected, because no one knew where else to put it; the stacked marble tiles, stone planters, broken tables—all these things were there for the same reason, he supposed. "Really, you have a large closet," he said, "with one wonderful window." The inner wall had two small openings with removable covers—"not so wonderful"—that looked down into a lecture hall. "Originally," Josef said, "a camera was operated from in here—people were surreptitiously observed." The door to my office was at the top of a stairway that came up from the building's main foyer—a handsome, almost elegant stairway you'd sooner expect in a castle.

One day I went looking for Josef but he wasn't around. Monika, the English department's young blonde secretary, greeted me as she often did: "Oh, my English! No good!" On the bulletin board I noticed the results of a contest for the best student essay written in English. The winner was from nearby Poprad. I looked at his picture—he was wearing a tuxedo—and then read his essay, which was printed underneath. He said, "Although the great majority of Slovaks wish to keep the Federation, they will do nothing about it. They will let the nationalist fanatics have their way." I asked Monika, "Have you read this?"

"Of course."

"Is it true?"

"Yes, of course."

"But why is it true?"

She rolled her eyes. "For me, no politics. I like young people—for example this handsome boy in the picture—who I hope will continue to be handsome—and cooking and—and how do you call it?—computers. Also psychology!"

Monika's bubbly friend Mary, a secretary in the geography department, on the floor below, came in. "Mary," I said, "can you help me find a map of Slovakia? None of the stores seems to have one."

"Slovakia? Oh, la-la, I wonder."

"Yes, yes, we can do that," Monika said, taking my hand. "Tomorrow! For now, join with us and enjoy cigarette, yes?" She patted my hand. Her long nails were pearl-colored; Madonna's face was printed everywhere on her blouse. I thanked them, no. Monika let go of my hand to answer the telephone. She spoke rapidly in Slovak, laid the phone on her desk, came back and seized my hand again. All of this caused Mary to bubble more. "Yes," Monika said, "you must sit!" Mary sat in a chair to show me how. They were flirting, we all knew it, and meanwhile the phone lay on the desk.

"Your call," I pointed.

Mary popped up, fired mock-serious-secretarial Slovak into the phone, then laid it down and returned to our little meeting. I had to laugh; they did too, Monika patting my hand, Mary showing me how to sit, the caller, perhaps a friend of theirs, perhaps also laughing, and why not? Who could imagine such silliness under the old system? But what about the young man from Poprad, his essay, his warning against apathy? Oh him, yes. His English is very good! Very. And how nice he looks in his tuxedo, like on TV. Then Lizzie showed up in her baseball cap and aviator's scarf, and Monika said, "Here is your woman!" They greeted each other; the bubbly meeting was now larger. The phone was still on the desk, still connected, a voice escaping tiny and tinny, and Monika produced a Czech-English dictionary to find a good word that would help us continue—

"Pages and pages! This book is so big!"

Josef and Anna's flat was basically like ours except the furniture was nicer and there were many books and pictures. "We have been here," Josef said, "seventeen years." He laughed. "I won't tell you where we lived before, I can't bear to remember it." Anna served soup made with fresh morels picked from the nearby woods. They gave us the best seats, so we could see the central yard—where grass and trees had been planted, years ago, to help soften the near view—and then the woods beyond. The hardwoods were turning red and yellow.

Nicole was not there. She had got up at five that morning to dig carrots in the country for spending money. She would earn a hundred crowns for a full day, Josef said. "A grand sum," Anita smiled, letting us know she didn't think it worth the effort. She had returned that fall from living a year in Connecticut on a government scholarship—one of only three high school students in all of Czechoslovakia to receive such a grant—and now she knew, even more than before, what things were worth. Her sweatshirt said OXFORD; she planned to be an academic like her parents.

Anna brought out a casserole of chicken breasts and paprikas and cheese. "Our lunch," she said. "But Josef will have vegetables and rice."

"I have three guardian angels watching everything I eat," he said.

“Nicole is the worst,” Anna laughed, “and so sharp-tongued about it! She caught him drinking coffee at the university the other day and practically made a speech.”

“Yes, Nicole is my sharpest critic.”

“As sharp as any you’ve had,” Anna shook her head.

Josef had to laugh. “I was thinking recently about those Kennedy books that got me in dutch.”

“What happened?” Lizzie asked.

“Typical nonsense,” he said. “A boring story. But humorous in a way.”

“Humorous is hardly the word,” Anna said.

“I had library duty in those days, in addition to my teaching,” Josef said. “Six copies of *Profiles in Courage* arrived—the U.S. Embassy in Prague sent them—and I put them in the library. A young colleague, who was in the Party, saw them and at his monthly meeting stood up and said to the Party chief—a man, incidentally, whose IQ I don’t believe could be measured it was so low—a real, a real, well, a real dumb man. Anyway, this young colleague—”

“Who is still on the faculty,” Anna broke in.

“Yes, yes, that’s all right,” Josef said to her. “Anyway, he said to his chief that copies of a book written by the imperialist John Kennedy were in the library, and he wondered if faculty member Grmela was ideologically ripe enough to be responsible—”

“Ideologically rigid enough you mean,” Anna corrected.

“What did I say?”

“You said ‘ripe.’”

“Oh well,” he laughed, “I must be reaching for something. In any case, this Party boss decided to freeze my salary and take away my course, American literature, my specialty, because I was not rigid enough.” He sighed. “But you know, Anna, really we all compromised ourselves to one degree or another. No one is untouched."

"He is too generous," she told us. "Even as a student he paid."

"No, no," he protested, "that's too far back, it's ancient history."

"You should tell them."

"I have said enough. I will sound like a crybaby, if I don't already."

Anna said, "When Josef was a student in Prague, at the School of Economics, he got caught listening to Radio Free Europe. They expelled him. Made him work for six years as a clerk before he could enroll again."

"A lucky thing," he sighed. "I would have made a lousy economist—the country would be even worse off than now."

Anita pointed out that the sun had left the yard but was still brilliant in the woods beyond.

"Yes, a walk," Josef declared. "Under the common trees with us!"

Outside, Anna said he should have been a forester. "I will use my next life with great pleasure," he said, "perhaps sampling one of those lookout towers in the American West—pondering such expressions as 'pardner' and wearing a ten-gallon hat."

Anita smiled. "My father has been to Pittsburgh."

"Yes," he said, "I was there in 'eighty-nine, during the revolution. But you see the kind of luck I have? Every time I go away something nice happens," he joked.

"They only let you go finally," Anna said, "because they knew something bad was about to happen and they wanted to be on your good side."

"The truth is, Anna, we do not know why they let me go abroad. My guess is a bureaucratic blunder. By the way," he said to me, "I am suddenly reminded that you are having a bureaucratic experience regarding your residence cards. Let me just say—then we can enjoy our walk—that it is not necessary for you to possess such cards. It is only necessary that you apply for them. As long as you are engaged in the application process you are within the law—even if the process takes forever. All you need is to be strong when matters become absurd."

"We should go to the castle," Anita said. "For some romance."

I walked beside her. "You must have deer in these woods," I said.

"We used to have a lot, but now there are none. The Communists shot one whenever they liked. My girlfriend ate deer tongue so often she got bored with it."

At Šariš Castle fog clung to the ruins. We climbed a long stone stairway, dodged trees growing through walls, and stopped on a grassy plateau in the lee of a leaning turret. "The former cake," I said. "Yes," Anita smiled, opening her backpack. "But I have real cake—apple cake—made from an old Moravian peasant recipe that's still dependable."

I thought of my Polish grandmother and of sitting with my chin on the oilcloth covering her kitchen table, with its waxy, leathery, vinegary smell, and then smelling the fresh coffee cake she brought from the oven that changed everything.

Lizzie took pictures of us in the fog and then we started down a path leading to Šariš village. We heard a rifle shot. Maybe, I said to Anita, there was one deer left. She said no, it was probably a rabbit. Before we got to the village, Josef pointed toward a cluster of Gypsy shanties in the trees. I thought of the fluid earth-colored drawings in a children's book Lizzie brought home in which trees might be animals and animals might be people and people might be trees again, but you had to look close.

Documents

That official in Prague who had advised against taking the train to Slovakia gave me six documents, and said, "When you are settled in Prešov, ask the university to sign and stamp these. Then take them to the police, along with photos of you and your wife, plus your passports, yes? This procedure will produce your residence cards. There is really nothing to it. The police are expecting you—these documents originated in their department." All the while she had that lost-filling expression.

A week or so later, in Prešov, I went to Igor's office. I found him busy with Monika and my colleague Nadia—they were counting a shipment of British grammars for Igor's private bookstore, a sideline he ran in a partitioned space in the building's main foyer. They were sipping wine and counting books and talking fast among themselves in Slovak.

I said, "*Dobrý den*"—hello—and showed Igor my documents.

He sighed, showing me his gap-toothed smile. "Very well then."

We went to the president's office, where three secretaries sat at a round table having coffee and smoking. Igor said something and they, taking turns, said something rather lengthy back to him. Then the women looked out the window; for several minutes no one spoke; the smoke in the room got thicker. What were we waiting for? One of the women glanced at me—the first acknowledgment, as far as I could tell, that I was among them. Finally another woman—a severe-looking blonde—stubbed out her cigarette and stood up. She searched in a desk and produced a rubber stamp, which she tested on a blank pad. She thumped it hard. She seemed put out at having to do this. Then without looking up she held a hand in our direction.

"The papers," Igor said. I gave them to him, he handed them to her, and she stamped them—thumping each one a little harder, I thought. When that was finished, Igor spoke again. "*Ano, ano*"—yes, yes—she sighed. She found a pen—another chore that seemed to annoy her—and signed the papers. Igor thanked her extravagantly—"*dejkuem, dejkuem*"—and we left. In the hall he got up on the balls of his feet, gave me the toothy smile and the papers, and winked, as if we had just pulled off a very smooth deal.

At the police station the official who handled residence cards was a woman with purple hair. The way it sat puffed on her skull made me think of fake Easter basket grass. The dye job wasn't complete—you could see at least two inches of yellow root.

"*Dobrý den,*" I said.

She said, "*Prosím,*" which meant *please* and was a word used to begin almost any kind of transaction—with a shop clerk, a waiter, a stranger you stopped on the street for directions. Here it meant for me to state my business. I laid my six documents on her desk.

She commenced to read them. She barely moved—she seemed to become transfixed. When at one point she made a deep sigh, I felt a sharp urge to ask, *What made you do that?* I kept quiet, standing in front of her desk. There was a chair I might have used, but she hadn't invited me to sit down—which was fine, I figured this wouldn't take long. She read on, absently twisting a gold pinkie ring. Her fingers were thick as breakfast sausages, and she wore rings on all of them, including the thumbs.

Finally she finished. I laid photos of Lizzie and me and then our passports on her desk. I didn't mean to exactly, but I laid them down with little snaps, like playing cards.

She glanced at them. Then up at me. Then—not returning my smile—she stared straight ahead. A minute must have passed.

I said, "*Nerozumím.*" I don't understand.

Slowly she rose from her chair, a large woman pushing up with both palms flat on her desk and sighing; the mass of purple hair tilted forward. At a file cabinet she pulled out three drawers. Whatever she wanted wasn't in them. On the wall above the cabinet hung a large color portrait of President Vaclav Havel. Well, that would be gone soon.

Back at her desk she opened a drawer and removed a form. On a piece of paper she wrote two or three sentences in a surprisingly pretty, filigreed script—and handed both the form and the message to me, saying "*Univerzita.*"

"You want me to take these to the university?"

She returned everything I had given her, pointed at the door, and nodded.

Her note instructed me to fill out a new personal history form. I learned this from Nadia, the only member of the English department I could find when I returned there. It was absurd, Nadia said, because the old form and the new were practically the same. A couple of items were in different places, that was all.

But with Nadia's help I filled out the new form, telling again who I was, who my parents and siblings were, where we were all born and lived and worked—including complete birth dates and street addresses and addresses of employers—and whether or not I was married and had children and where my wife and children were born, lived, and worked.

"There," Nadia said, "that should satisfy your friend. But please, on your next visit to the police take me with you."

I said I was going to be in Slovakia all year and needed to be a big boy.

"Like John Wayne maybe? Coffee?" She heated water in an electric pot. Her office was a bright cheerful room with a vase of dried flowers on the desk and colorful posters on all the walls—including one of Mount Rushmore. I felt a wave of nostalgia. I thought I could even smell sagebrush, popcorn, and mustard, and turning my gaze from Washington, Jefferson, Roosevelt, and Lincoln I almost expected to see a row of hot dogs bursting open on a vender's spit in the South Dakota sunshine.

"Are you okay?" Nadia said.

"Sure, things are fine."

"The wonderful American word *sure*."

"I know what I did wrong."

"Yes? How interesting."

"I was not polite."

“Yes, we must behave like perfect children in certain situations.”

“If I do exactly as she wishes, how can there be any screw-up?”

“Oh, well,” Nadia said, raising her hands, “it is quite, *quite* possible.”

I was eating a sausage with sauerkraut in the university café. Josef appeared. “I’m glad I found you,” he said. “Will you be ready, say in fifteen minutes, to meet your Fourth Year students? They are waiting.”

“I thought I was scheduled to begin tomorrow?”

“That’s true. But they are here now, as you are, so why not? I can make a few introductory remarks, then you can tell them your plans for this year.”

“What areas are they weak in?”

“They are the last class admitted to the university before the revolution—not an exemplary group. How is your lunch?”

“It’s a good hot dog. Now I want to see the World Series. What do you know about baseball, Josef?”

“Very little. In Pittsburgh they are called the Pirates.”

“And the students?”

“Excuse me, what is your question?”

“What do they know about baseball?”

“Oh, well, I have no idea. Probably as little as I do.”

“Maybe that’s where I should begin.”

He chuckled—obviously I was joking—then got back to business. He thought they would like the stories of Poe and Washington Irving. “And of course several have read translations of Dreiser and Hemingway, whose works were available under the old regime.”

“How are they on poetry?”

“I fear poetry—ah, I see you have finished your hot dog—will be difficult for them.”

I followed him to a lecture hall that was next to Igor's private bookshop and close to my office. I said, "I'll be right with you." I went up to my office and got the baseball I'd brought from the States.

Josef was standing behind the lectern when I rejoined him, speaking to the students in Slovak. Seeing me he switched to English. With considerable formality in gesture and tone he introduced me, then bowing like a waiter he went out.

About forty students, most of them women, sat in five or six ascending rows, their notebooks ready. It occurred to me that I was beginning my last year of teaching. I felt loose, relaxed. I walked along the first row tossing my ball up and catching it.

"Do you know what this thing is?" I asked.

The faces were sober, non-committal.

"Any idea?"

Two women in a middle row smiled to each other. I pointed at them. "Take a guess."

They shook their heads as if they had bees in their hair.

"What does it look like?" I held up the ball.

More head shakes.

"Get ready," I said, "here it comes." I lobbed the ball at the one with the biggest smile. It landed with a bang on the writing shelf in front of her. She squealed, catching it on the bounce in both hands. Her face beamed. I applauded.

"Now," I said, "what do you have?"

All she could do was shake her head and hold the ball tightly as if it were a bird she had captured.

"What is your name?" I asked.

"Eva."

"So you *can* speak to me."

"Of course."

"What do you think you're holding?"

"In my opinion a kind of ball."

"Can you describe it?"

"Oh, it is quite strong. And loud too, I think."

A few of us laughed.

"It's not loud now, is it?"

"No," she said, "because I am keeping it quiet."

More laughter—okay—we were all getting loose.

"You are holding a baseball, Eva."

"I know."

"You know?"

"Yes, I have seen it in the film *The Natural.*"

"Then why didn't you say so earlier?"

"Maybe I was waiting for you to tell us."

"What if I told you that the game of baseball will help you understand America and therefore American literature?"

A number of students began to write in their notebooks. But a guy in the front row, I noticed, sat hunched over staring at his palms as if life were an emptiness and he too.

"Eva, please toss me the ball." She did. "Good throw." I rolled it along the front row writing shelf toward the guy. The ball stopped next to his hands. He didn't touch it. Slowly he looked up at me.

"And what is your name?" I asked.

"I am Vlado."

"Do you know who Joe DiMaggio is, Vlado?"

"He is mentioned by Simon and Garfunkel," Vlado said.

"Yes—and also by Hemingway in *The Old Man and the Sea.* Santiago, fighting the sharks for his marlin, gets to thinking about the great DiMaggio."

Vlado simply looked at me.

"Joe DiMaggio was an exceptional baseball player. He was strong and graceful and he made the difficult appear easy."

"Like Superman," Vlado said without humor.

I figured I would like this guy Vlado.

"Most of the time Joe failed," I said, now speaking to everyone. "That's how it is in baseball—that's the beautiful thing about the game—how often you are allowed to fail."

The faces before me seemed to say maybe they were in the wrong room.

"American literature," I said, "has a lot of stuff in it—Puritans, cowboys, rivers, jazz, cars, the open road and advertising and ghettos and suburbia and farms—because America is all over the place. It's both busy and lonely, it's a grab bag, it collects and piles up and grooms and throws away and wants more. It wants to look good and in its best moments be good. Hitch your wagon not to a horse, Emerson said, but to a star. It's a country of romance and dreams and that big juicy carrot Success. We're crazy about success, we think about it almost all the time. We can't help pursuing it. But it's our beautiful failures that really describe us."

I glanced around at the eyes avoiding me.

"Okay, its early—and we're just getting started." I looked at Vlado.

"Games," he said, "are for boys." He picked up the ball and held it out to me. It wasn't anything, his expression said, that he cared to spend more time on.

I returned to the police station with my fresh personal history form, but Grape Hair was not in. A clerk told me, "Maybe Monday."

At the university I went looking for my Requalifiers. These were former teachers of Russian who were being retooled to teach English: every Friday they came to the university from all over eastern Slovakia, women mainly, from their late twenties to their fifties, Viera and Adja, Rut and Xenia and Alzbeta, they are called, but I haven't met them yet because I can't find room 70. I find 68, 69, and 71, how can 70 not be there? The slip of paper Monika gave me shows three meetings with this group: two seminars with half the group in each, and then a lecture to all—and the times 11:30, 14:40, 15:25—but none of this can start without room 70.

I stop a student. "I am looking for room 70."

"It is very simple," she says, and begins counting off. Aha! She too is puzzled. "Moment," she says; she will inquire at a *kľúč* lady's kiosk. *Kľúč* means *key;* all classrooms are locked and one must go to a *kľúč* lady and ask for the relevant key. I know this but haven't picked up that rhythm yet.

The student returns. "No key," she says.

"How about a room?" I ask.

"A room? But if there is no key, how can there be a room?"

"You mean no key exists?"

"There is no—what is it called? Where you hang the key?"

"Hook?"

"Precisely, no hook. Therefore no key, no room. A pity."

A middle-aged woman in a babushka approaches and speaks rapid Slovak to the student, pointing down the hall. The student says, "*Ano, ano.*" The woman leaves, shaking her head.

"The *kľúč* lady," the student says. "She solves our problem. Come."

I follow the student to an open doorway. "There," she says. I look in—it's a large room whose walls are lined with urinals. "Room 70," she says.

I return to the English department. Monika is on the phone, but sets it down. I show her the paper she'd given me. "Room 70 is a toilet," I say.

"Really? A toilet?" She picks up the phone, fires off some Slovak—including the word *toaleta*—laughs "*ano, ano,*" then sets the phone down and consults a ledger on her desk. "Hmmm, try room 25. Much nicer. *Ciao!*"

I go there—it's a science lab with sinks and foot-tall water spigots at all the tables—and find half my Requalifiers. They are eating their sack lunches and waiting for me to discuss the lecture I am scheduled to give later that day.

Nights, cooking dinner, we tuned in the Voice of America on our Russian-made shortwave radio. We heard the Glenn Miller orchestra, we heard Winston Churchill's gravelly assurances, we heard Jo Stafford sing "Kiss me once, kiss me twice, and kiss me once again. . . ." Lizzie sang along. I saw my uncles Joe and Johnny in uniform, and pretty women in wide-brimmed hats lifting that fine netting away from their faces to fix impressions of their lips on my cheek. They were leaving on long journeys or just coming back, and if I saw tears I also heard laughter and nothing, ever, the laughter said, could be very bad. I loved the smell of wool and perfume and after-shave, the expression "GI," the word "overseas," the wail of a saxophone. I listened to Lizzie and Jo sing "I'll be seeing you in all the old familiar places. . . ." On those nights when the clear, close, brilliant moon slipped down from the Tatras and hung over our kitchen balcony, we would step out there and dance in its light. "Where are we, Doctor G.?"

I finally found Grape Hair and gave her my papers. She took her time checking everything out. Then she gave it all back to me.

"*Nerozumím,*" I said.

She said nothing. From her desk she produced another new form for me. No accompanying note this time. She didn't even point to the door and say "*Univerzita.*"

Walking down the hall toward the English department I saw Nadia, but her expression was not happy.

"How are you?" I said.

"Fine," she said, the skin around her eyes a bruised color.

I almost said, "Are you sure?" but I only smiled and kept going, saying nothing about Grape Hair's new form.

Josef's door opened before I knocked on it.

"Please," he said, "if you have a moment."

I went in, sat down.

"Everything," he said, "has gotten worse since the revolution. All the Communists in the bureaucracy managed to keep their jobs. Add them to the newcomers and the result is more forms to fill out. After all, everyone's job must be important."

"This is uncanny, Josef. I just came from the police with yet another new form."

"What is uncanny about it? Nothing could be more normal."

"How are things with you?"

"I must go to Bohemia."

I waited to hear more, but he waved the subject away. He began packing a briefcase. I stood up, wishing him a good journey. "Yes," he sighed, "we'll see what they can divine."

That afternoon, walking to the department store in town to buy a water filter, I saw Anna rushing along the street. I caught up with her.

"I just put Josef on the train," she said, almost out of breath. "Now I'm trying to catch my bus."

"He's going to Bohemia?"

"Oh, the poor man. He's so embarrassed about it. Because he *looks* so healthy, doesn't he? Ruddy, robust. But what can we do? I must run—there's my bus. Please give Elizabeth our love."

The next time I went to meet my Fourth Year students in the lecture room near Igor's bookshop, I found them waiting outside the closed door.

"Shall we go in?" I said.

"Someone is in there," said Eva, my catcher.

"Isn't this our room now?" I said.

"Maybe we can find another room," she suggested timidly.

"Who's in there?" I asked her.

"We don't know," she said.

I tried the door. It was locked.

"Did anyone go for the key?"

"The key has been taken," she told me, "presumably by those inside. Maybe it's a special situation. We can go over there today, if you like." She pointed to the courtyard, which had several pieces of outdoor sculpture and some benches.

"I do like," I said.

So we went there and pulled benches together. I gave them cards to write down their names and the titles of any American stories, poems, or novels they'd read.

"Zuzana Amanova," I said, "you have listed Stephen King and *Gone with the Wind* and Edgar Allan Poe. Tell us your impressions of a Poe story."

She was small and dark and needed a moment to compose herself. "Poe," she finally said, "was an author who took drugs. Also he married his young cousin. I believe she was only thirteen."

"Can you say anything about Poe's stories?"

"I read these works a long time ago, I'm afraid."

"Tatiana Drobnakova. You also mention Mr. King and Miss Mitchell, but the best book you list is *An American Tragedy.* Can you talk about it?"

"Of course," she smiled. "Dreiser was a famous naturalist. He saw much poverty and selfishness. He had twelve brothers and sisters who drank a lot and had children without two parents."

"You're telling me about the author, not the novel," I said.

She blushed and looked at her hands.

"Eva Zelena," I called.

"That's me."

"What does Zelena mean?"

"I am green," she laughed.

"The color of dollars."

"Also the strong part of a flower."

"Better yet. Now, you've read *Catch-22*."

"Joseph Heller, the author, worked many years in advertising. He—"

"Hold on," I interrupted. "Tell about the novel."

"It was very long. It was about, in my opinion, how crazy are some U.S. soldiers. But I believe war can make anybody crazy, in my opinion."

"Thank you. Vlado Bucko—did I pronounce that right?"

"*Bootch*ko," he said.

"You've read quite a lot, it looks like, including *The Old Man and the Sea*. What is your opinion of that novel?"

"Hemingway," he said, "had great sympathy for ordinary workers, and for men in difficulties. He himself was often injured and described such conditions, for example, in *A Farewell to Arms*. Santiago, by the way, does not remember Joe DiMaggio in my copy of this book."

"He doesn't?"

"I looked and there is no mention."

"That's impossible."

"You may see for yourself." He handed me the book.

"This is in Slovak."

"Yes."

"So your translator deleted the Yankee Clipper," I said.

"It proves that baseball is not necessary for an understanding of this story," Vlado said.

"But you're not getting the whole story," I told him. Then to the others: "I'm not hearing much about story at all. Mainly I'm hearing about the authors' lives. Why is that?"

No one offered to tell me, so I turned up a new card.

"Beata Kovalova, would you tell me?"

She was a thin blonde with high cheekbones and startling eyes, a wolf's eyes. She said, "This is information we have been taught."

"How is this information useful?"

"For our exams," she said.

"Should I give you such information?"

"Yes, of course."

"And when we have our exam you will recite it back to me."

"Yes."

"We would be like two parrots."

"That's how it is done," Beata said.

"If you were a medical student and I a surgeon I would tell you please memorize the location of the appendix in relation to the heart so that you do not confuse them one day. But you are not a medical student."

"Still," she said, "isn't it true that we need facts?"

"Name a few important facts we need to live our lives—in your opinion."

"I'm sorry, I can only think of food."

There was laughter. She blushed. I was about to quote William Carlos Williams' poem about the plums in the icebox—to support her, and to try to introduce expression, the human back-and-forth, into our discussion—but they started gathering up their things.

"We must say good-bye," Eva smiled. "We have gymnastic now."

Lizzie and I returned to the woods below Šariš Castle. We found the path we had taken with the Grmelas, and we saw the Gypsy town again—shanties that appeared woven out of growing trees and scrap lumber and tin and broken bricks, made of anything the Gypsies could scavenge. The shanties lay close to the Torysa River. No one could say how many Gypsies lived there, but we were advised not to use that part of the path after dark, or at all if we could help it. We saw their wood fires, the late sun catching tin roofs as dusk came on, and then ahead of us half a dozen children jumping back and forth across the path as if it were hot.

We watched them. We both thought of the book Lizzie had brought home—the story of a witch snatching a child from his parents and flying with him to the woods, the wonderful drawings showing all kinds of animals looking on and dancing. Those drawings, we thought, could have come directly from this place, these woods.

When the children saw us they froze almost dead still—staring wide-eyed as if we each possessed two heads. "Hello," I said. They turned their backs to us, and we walked by.

A week later we returned, and again, as if in a recurring dream, we found the children jumping across the path ahead of us. This time they watched us go by with sidelong glances over their shoulders. When we got fifteen or twenty feet past them, we heard an owl-hoot, a dog-yip, and turning to look, we saw a bold pair race toward us wildly waving their arms. They pulled up short, whirled, and showed us their backs. We continued walking. The boldest child then raced past us a dozen feet, stopped, and watched us go by, his eyes cut back over his shoulder. Another child joined the game, and another, until we had nine or ten of them racing ahead of us, stopping, and standing like sentries—or an honor guard—at intervals along the path. They were all small and dark and very limber, very quick, and had beautiful eyes.

When we came to a place where the river narrowed and the edge of Šariš village appeared, the child who had started this game grinned as if we might speak now.

"What are you called?" I asked. "Your name? *Meno?*"

Grinning, the boy jumped onto a large stone at the river's edge. He snatched up a small branch floating by and hurled it downstream in a great arc that pleased him. He then crossed the river on stones that had been placed there for that purpose or had been there forever—leaping graceful as a deer—and disappeared.

An art student named Juraj came to my office one Friday and asked to join my Fourth Year class. He was soft-spoken, dark, slightly built, and very polite; his English was good, but he seemed to choose his words so carefully I got the feeling he was afraid that if he chose the wrong word it might blow up in his face. I said I would be happy to have him join the class. He bowed and left.

He returned to my office later when I was through teaching for the day. Lizzie was also there, finishing up a drawing. He said to us, "Please, if you don't mind, call me George." He brought along a fellow art student named Mikel, also soft-spoken but not nearly so careful as George to choose his words. Would we like to see the art department?

"When?" Lizzie said.

"It is free now," Mikel said, "if that is convenient."

They took us to a section of the building, a first-floor level, whose hallway was completely dark. They felt along the wall for a light switch, going ahead of us. Mikel laughed, "Don't be afraid!" Finally the hallway lit up. Along its length, except in the spaces for doors, hung drawings of human figures, in charcoal on rough brown paper. At first I thought of the Gypsy children in the woods; but these drawings of mainly large heads on stick-like bodies had no playfulness in their faces, only strain, as if someone had pulled at their mouths and eyes to stretch them into permanent grotesqueries.

"A recent exhibition," Mikel said without further comment.

George opened a door. "In here are models, if you care to look."

"Yes, they are made here," Mikel said.

Dozens of white plaster heads sat on a wall of shelves, all of the heads lined up to face out. They seemed identical, like mannequin heads used in a department store to display hats. The only variation came from the depth of shadow in the empty eye sockets.

I thought of the essay by the student from Poprad warning against apathy. I asked if George and Mikel knew of it. They said of course. After a moment, Mikel said, "We behaved under Socialism. The Czechs also were complacent, but they have a lot of German influence and know how to be aggressive."

George held up a picture he found leaning against the wall—a paper collage showing Czechoslovakia in the form of a banana half-peeled. "You will notice," he said, "it's the Czech part that's peeled."

We were quiet. Then Lizzie said, trying for a cheerful note, "Gary and I were on the bus the other day, laughing about something silly, and a woman suddenly handed me an apple just before she got off."

"Yes," Mikel said, "she would like to join you. It's like this—the first year of the revolution was wonderful, people on the buses talked with each other, made plans, you never heard this before. The second year was a little less wonderful, and now, I'm afraid, your woman with the apple is rare."

As we were leaving the building, George said, "My father has been an artist all his life. Tomorrow he is showing new work. Will you come?"

The show was at a gallery in Prešov's historical section—in a renovated eighteenth-century shop—and it was an elegant affair. A cellist in a black gown played Haydn sonatas. Champagne was served, fresh flowers set out. George's father, also called Juraj, was an older version of the son, soft-spoken and very polite, except that his close-cut hair was pure white and he was permanently bent over. He bowed to us and kissed Lizzie's hand. "Please," he said, his large dark eyes watery bright, "enjoy yourselves." A woman followed us when Lizzie and I went to look at the pictures, and said, "You know of course he is well thought of. His pictures decorate many public buildings. They are old-fashioned, yes, but still a tribute." She owned the gallery, she said, and was proud to be part of his—what was the word?—rebirth?

The pictures were mainly landscapes of mountains executed with blocks of rich color; two or three were portraits of children. One was of George as a boy. They were all pleasant to look at, all handsomely framed, and all of them, as Lizzie said later, made you want to cry. If you had never seen Van Gogh's or Cezanne's pictures, they would have been spectacular.

A few days after this show, George invited us to see the Andy Warhol Museum in Medzilaborce, near the Polish border; he took us there in the family Lada—a small Russian-made car named for a sprite in Slovak folklore. George was quiet for much of the drive. Then he said, "Not long ago a newspaper in Prague listed everyone in Czechoslovakia who was with the secret police. My uncle's name was there. We had no idea. Also several English department faculty. Some were to be expected. But Nadia and Slavka and Josef shocked us."

Lizzie and I said nothing.

"Initially," George said, "I felt that my admiration for these people had been betrayed. But I gave the matter thought. They must have been compromised in some small way. Perhaps they wanted to leave the country, for a conference, and in order to go were given a document to sign. It meant nothing—a stupid paper, nothing more. My father for example wanted to visit Italy. He would sign nothing, but a member of the police traveled with him—everywhere—as if he were blind. This is how it was."

In Medzilaborce we walked to the museum across a square that had been decorated three years before by children. "Yes," George said, "they were given cans of white paint and brushes. You can see the result." We saw goofy faces and bursting suns and other such figures on the cement.

George came to class faithfully for about a month, sitting near Vlado usually, and never said anything unless I called on him. He was even more careful choosing his words in front of a group. Then he stopped attending class. During the rest of that year we would see him in town from time to time; he would apologize for missing class and always promise to return soon.

Expression

"How are you?" I said to Nadia.

"Fine," and she looked at her dried flowers, at the posters of Vienna and Mount Rushmore on her office wall. "Yes, every day when you ask how I am, I say fine because that is the expected response."

"On a scale from one to ten, how are you?"

"I will teach you something. To a Slovak most days are bad. However, some days we might feel that things are not so bad but could be better. And once in a great while they are okay. That is our scale."

I went to meet my Requalifiers. Using English, especially when responding to me in front of their peers, was difficult for them. "We don't want to sound stupid," Zenia said. "After all, we are teachers." I kept praising their efforts and challenging them, and in the way, more or less, that a rusty nut can be unbound with oil and a wrench, they began to loosen up.

Drahomira Dragonova ("Call me Dada, maybe is easier for you") was an exception. She was a professor of philosophy at the university and married to the former dean of ideology, whom the students, in the first heady days of revolution, demanded be canned. The position was canned, too. Dada remained. She sat in the first row and needed no invitation to speak. (She put me in mind of Yogi Berra, not for her dipsy-doodle syntax—there was no accidental poetry in it—but for the shape of her jaw.) If she got stuck in English, she'd fire off what she meant in Slovak and snap her fingers for a translation. Someone always provided it. No matter whom we discussed—Hawthorne, Twain, Dickinson, Welty—Dada wanted to nail his or her "philosophy," summarize it in a sentence. When I called for further comments, other ways of describing Hawthorne's or Welty's view of humanity, Dada's eyes would narrow and her jaw clench. It was hard for her to entertain the notion that writers, or the characters and dramas they created, were larger or more complex than a simple declarative sentence, especially if the sentence has just come from her. I became fond of the Slovak expression *za'bada,* which means "a mystery." For example, why was Dada—who did not conduct her philosophy courses in English—taking my American literature class? When I asked, she threw me an interesting curve. "*Kde je pes zakopaný*," she said. It meant, literally, "Where the dog is buried." Or, as Slovak friends would tell me, "Where the truth begins."

Josef was standing outside his office, having just returned from Bohemia (where, I'd learned from Anna, he'd gone for a special kidney treatment).

"I'm happy to see you back, Josef."

"As a man pommeled by science, I share your happiness."

"But you look fine, you really do."

"If I am left alone I feel normal, though I am told I should feel otherwise. How is Elizabeth? How are you? Have the police given you your residence cards yet?"

"We're fine—and the cards, well, that's a story in progress."

He invited me into his office and closed the door. "The police," he said. "You know, last summer Anna my wife, running across the street, in the rain, to catch a bus, is struck by a car. Her collarbone is knocked out of line, ribs are bruised, nylon stockings ruined—but *prosím, prosím,* she mumbles, regaining consciousness, it is her fault, not the driver's, she simply wasn't paying attention under her umbrella."

He pulled at his beard. "She visits the police station as required and gives her report, absolving the driver. Yet months later the police are still investigating. Today, in fact, at an early hour, they took Anna to the scene of the accident, stopped all traffic in the center of town, made lines with chalk, occupied their stations, gave the signal, and sent her back across the street, at a run, to re-enact the moment before the car struck her. The police held stopwatches, were timing her for some reason known only to themselves. Over and over they sent this unathletic, middle-aged professor of British literature running across the street, timing her, refining their art, I suppose, until at length she falls and ruins another pair of nylon stockings. She also bloodied her elbows and knees. We can't help but feel she is under suspicion, but for what?"

After a moment, I said, "Josef, I'm sorry."

"Nothing could be more normal."

"Would you and your family have Thanksgiving dinner with us?"

"An honor. I remember my first Thanksgiving, in Pittsburgh. I became stuffed, like the turkey."

"Maybe we can stuff you again."

"Speaking of stuffing, I have a note regarding your flat. It seems the rent is not being paid."

I asked him why not.

"Well, it seems you are not paying it."

"The university is, isn't it?"

"Unfortunately, no."

I mentioned his letter to me before I left the States in which he said I would receive a monthly salary of 5,000 crowns plus a rent allowance. "Since I've been getting my salary but no rent allowance, I assumed," I said, "that the university has been paying the rent."

"I'm afraid not."

"What happened to the allowance?"

He didn't really know. That rent allowance phrase, he said, had been given to him by the authorities in Bratislava and he dutifully passed it along to me in his letter.

"Maybe we should write to Bratislava and ask what's going on?"

"We can do that," he said, "but I am not confident it will do any good. I am confident they will direct me to handle the situation from here."

"I'm puzzled, Josef."

"It is logical for you to be puzzled. It is also fair for you to assume that I, as dean of international affairs, should know more about the content of my letters than I do. But alas I know very little."

He sighed and stared at the wall behind his desk. "All I know," he said, "is that we, here, provided you and Elizabeth with a flat, which is one of several the university has reserved for its purposes."

"But by 'provide' you don't mean 'pay for.'"

"That, unfortunately, is correct."

"So why haven't I received any bills?"

"You should have. According to the records"—he consulted a paper—"three bills have been prepared since September."

"For my address?"

"Yes."

"*Za'hada.*"

"You haven't received anything addressed to Victor Licorice? As you know, he was your predecessor at the university."

"Josef, why would I receive mail addressed to Victor Licorice?"

"Because the flat is registered in his name."

"Victor lived in my apartment?"

"No, he never actually lived there. It is only a one-bedroom flat and he had too many children. He lived across town in a two-bedroom flat."

"Why is the apartment registered in his name then?"

"It was just easier that way," Josef said.

"Easier than what?"

"Than not doing it that way."

"I see. Here is an apartment reserved for the university's purposes and registered in the name of an American who doesn't live there, who never lived there, doesn't even live in Slovakia anymore, though bills are sent out addressed to him there but really intended for the current occupant—me—who is just now having this novel system explained to him."

We gazed at the wall behind Josef's desk. An illustrated map of the U.S. hung there, a cartoonish badger meeting a cartoonish wolverine over the Great Lakes.

Finally he said, "Shall we say everything is cleared up?"

"That's a good line, Josef."

"Anna doesn't think I'm funny at all."

"If we say everything is clear, then what?"

"We can turn this entire matter over to Bozka, our keeper of such records. She will determine how much of the bill is your responsibility and how much is Victor's."

"You're still joking."

"It seems Victor left for the States still owing something."

"I won't ask why. Or why his bill and mine were tossed together."

"Good."

"Let's assume it was convenient, for whatever reason, to register that apartment in the name of a man who never lived there. But just between us, Josef, why does it continue to be registered in his name?"

"Gary," he said wearily, "to try and change anything now would cause such a mountain of paperwork, not to mention headache, ulcers, and constipation, that they might as well remove both my kidneys and forget about me."

"You don't need an operation?"

"A certain specialist, formerly a good Party member, seems eager to subtract one. I have decided to avoid him."

"Let me buy you a coffee," I said.

"You know I'm forbidden to drink it."

"Tea?"

"Also forbidden. Alcohol and fruit juice as well."

"Hot chocolate?"

"Never."

"So as things stand. . . ."

"So as things stand, it is possible to say that neither the man who officially lives in your flat, nor the man who in fact lives there, lives there."

"What *do* you drink, Josef?"

"I can't bear to describe it."

Slavka, the department's sunniest member, asked me how things were going. I told her I was in pursuit of residence cards and having some trouble, but otherwise things were going well.

"Really, no other problems?"

"Well, my Fourth Year students and I seem to have lost our lecture room. We meet in the courtyard."

"What will you do when it snows in earnest?"

"A question raised—timidly—by one or two."

"And how did you respond to them?"

"I said we would get close and recite Whitman. 'Smile O voluptuous cool-breath'd earth! Smile, for your lover comes.'"

"Your American humor. But tell me, seriously, what is the situation with regard to the residence cards?"

I showed her the police department's latest form to be filled out.

"It seems," she said, "they are requesting physical examinations."

I explained that Lizzie and I had complete physicals just before leaving the States—as required by the Fulbright office. "I have Xeroxes of the reports," I said.

"Good," Slavka said. "I think I should go with you to the police."

Feeling sheepish, I accepted her offer.

Grape Hair and Slavka had two very long exchanges, the official dominating. The gist of the first was that the police *might* accept the U.S. health reports. The question was whether the exams had been complete or only partial; partial was unacceptable. And, too, the reports were too old; thirty days seemed to be the limit and, as Grape Hair pointed out, our reports were dated three months ago. So she needed to phone someone in the ministry to obtain special approval, but the person who could grant such approval was not, Grape Hair knew, available at this hour.

The second long exchange concerned the subject of any criminal acts that I, or Lizzie, may have committed since arriving in Czechoslovakia. To begin the paperwork necessary to clear us of this or these possibilities, Grape Hair gave me a form that I needed to take downstairs to the police station coffee shop and, one, buy a special stamp for and, two, fill out with my complete personal history—also my wife's—and then, three, take to the main post office and mail to the Division of Criminal Investigation in Bratislava. If this form came back to me showing that Lizzie and I were clean, I could then bring it to Grape Hair's office for *her* stamp. At that time, also, she assured Slavka, her phone call to the ministry regarding the acceptance or refusal of the U.S. medical reports should have been completed and Lizzie and I would know where we stood on that question.

As Slavka translated, I kept my mouth shut. It wasn't easy. I wanted especially to point out that the medical reports had aged because Grape Hair sent me home with a new form to complete every time I came to call. Even Slavka's usual sunny aspect was darkened. But down in the coffee shop she brightened again. "Well"—smiling bravely—"everything will turn out fine. Would you care for a snack?"

The coffee shop was filling with clerks and liver-faced cops on their mid-morning breaks. We bought the special stamp I needed from the same woman who sold us coffee. Slavka guided me through the personal history form; except for an item or two in different locations, it was identical to all the others I had given the police. As I sat there keeping my mouth shut about that and about the need to be declared innocent, I saw Grape Hair come in. She bought three hot dogs. No bread, just the sausages. She sat at a table near ours and dipped her dogs, bite by bite, into a great pool of mustard.

A tall, slender woman in her thirties was waiting for me outside the Requalifiers classroom. "I missed your fall lectures because I was promised work in Canada. But now is no work. So I am here. I have everything. The big book, your assignments." Her voice seemed thinned by distance, like some I picked up on my shortwave radio. She had blonde hair waxed in a kind of rooster comb, red painted lips more vertical than horizontal—bright as a valentine—and light blue-gray eyes so still they seemed fake. Over a white turtleneck sweater she wore a black T-shirt that said in glittering green: KING OF THE DESERT.

"You are a Russian teacher?"

"Finished."

"What is your name?"

"I will write it."

I told Luba Baranova the fall lectures were not quite over and invited her in. She went to the back row, produced a notebook and pen, sat up straight, and fixed her eyes on me. Not once during class did her expression or position seem to change; she might have been posing for a long camera exposure. At one point I asked if she was following okay, and her eyes turned even flatter, as if I were trying to get more information out of her and she was unable to let that happen.

The next week she wore a T-shirt that said: U.S.A. YANKEE WINNER. The rooster comb hairdo, the valentine lips, the pen in hand, the stare—all the same. I tried another question—what, in her opinion, was the biggest lesson Huck Finn learned? The blue-gray eyes seemed to say: Please, I am here, isn't that enough?

On the last day before mid-year break, Luba approached me in the hall. HELLO HOLLYWOOD said this week's T-shirt. She held up her grade book, which resembled a passport; all students carried them.

"I request your signature," she said. "For my first semester credit. Or I will lose everything. I must have it today."

"Why today?"

"I pray you."

"Don't pray me. Explain."

The eyes didn't move. "I must," she said.

"Look, Luba, I am happy to help you. But why today?"

"My credit. I pray you."

"Okay, look. The day is young. We will meet later."

I went up to the English department to see what anyone knew about this woman. In Igor's office he had Monika and Nadia helping him count books for his private bookshop. They were into it like thieves. I knocked on Josef's door; no response. In my mind I could hear him say, "But surely the committee that devoted perhaps years to designing the system gave it serious thought." I found Slavka in, eating a cucumber. "My breakfast," she smiled. "I have been rushing all morning wondering where I am." She had the warmest smile of anyone I'd met in Slovakia, but now, hearing about Luba Baranova's request, she turned almost grim. "Yes, I know this situation. You may give her an exam or you may ask her to write an essay for the first semester credit."

"But why does she need a signature today?"

"Her problem is not your problem," Slavka said, then picked up some papers and said she had class. "Do what you think is best."

At the lecture Luba fixed her look on me, as always. I tried to gather up a few threads: a sense of place, the times they are a-changing, who am I? Near the end I went to the padded door and whacked it with my palm, quoting Whitman: "Unscrew the locks from the doors! / Unscrew the doors themselves from their jambs!" It opened. There stood Igor, smiling, up on the balls of his feet. He had the former Russian teachers now, for Didactic, his specialty.

I left. In the hall Luba was suddenly beside me.

"Relax," I said. "Don't you want to go to Igor's class?"

"My credit," she said.

"Okay. Five o'clock, in my office?" Meanwhile, I suggested, she might go somewhere quiet, perhaps the library, and prepare.

She shook her head. "No examination can be necessary, because look"—she showed me two pages of exquisite calligraphy detailing the basic facts of Stephen Crane's life, information she'd copied from her text.

"That's fine," I said, "but can you talk about something he wrote?"

"I pray you."

"Please, no praying. Go read. Something *by* Crane—anything—and we'll talk about it. Also anything by Thoreau."

"Thoreau avoided the capitalists."

"Good start. At five o'clock—"

"No five o'clock."

She was right beside me on the handsome stairway leading to my office. My back was aching. I needed a swim. The pool was open for faculty from four to five. It was quarter to four. I could hear her breathing.

"Okay," I said, stopping, "who is Huck Finn?"

"A little boy."

"Do you like him?"

"I don't understand."

"I don't understand this goofy system."

"I pray you."

"Please, Luba, go read something."

"'Song of Myself' is a poem by Walt Whitman." She looked at me as if the light had stunned her, maybe even hurt her, then held up her grade book again. I took it. At the front was a photo taken when she first entered the university, at eighteen or so. Her eyes were regular eyes, youthful, bright, and her lips almost smiled, not yet frozen into the neon heart she walked around with now.

"Listen," I said. "I *will* help you."

Her expression softened; she even glanced away and sighed.

"Good," I said. "So—go to the library and read some passages you can tell me about at five o'clock." I made to return the grade book, but she didn't want it; she wanted me to take her pen.

"Please, you can sign it now."

My neck was heating up. "Luba, are you listening?"

"Understand me."

"Understand you. Jesus. Where is the dog buried?"

I continued up the ornate handsome lousy stairs and opened my door. She was right beside me. She glanced around at Lizzie's new pastels on the walls. Then she walked to the piano. "Do you play?"

"No."

"But you have this nice instrument."

"It was just in here."

Suddenly she was seated, playing. Beautifully. Rochmaninoff. The room filled with gorgeous, round, passionate sound. What could be more important?

A Kind of Fable

Lizzie and I settle into our compartment on the Budapest Express, going to Bratislava. A six-hour ride in the new year—the year that the Slovaks and Czechs are officially divorced. We are happy to be leaving Prešov for a while.

I open my copy of *Tess of the D'Urbervilles,* and there is Thomas Hardy quoting Whitman: "Crowds of men and women attired in the usual costumes, / How curious you are to me!"

A young couple enters. "*Dobrý den,*" we all say. Good day. The newcomers each carry a large bottle of Coke; their jackets say LOS ANGELES on the back. They sit side by side. The man opens a book; the woman slings a leg over one of his and watches him read.

Lizzie and I sit across from each other next to the window. I try to follow Angel falling in love with Tess, but I'm distracted by the woman beside me stroking her companion's inner thigh. Finally he tells her to sit across from him. She sighs theatrically, feigning great disappointment, but moves away, taking a magazine from her tote bag. On its cover Madonna is almost bare-breasted, her hair, like Luba Baranova's, twisted in a rooster comb.

The train, brakes shrieking, stops in Ružomberok, and into our compartment step four young women with big red Nike duffel bags. The Madonna fan moves quickly next to her man. The tallest newcomer sits beside me, the others beside Lizzie. I say, "Basketball," and they all smile and say, "Basketball!" I introduce myself and Lizzie and explain that we are spending a year in Slovakia.

"And what is your opinion of our tiny country?"

"We have seen the Tatras, Slovenský Raj, Banská Bystrica—many places—and find them beautiful," Lizzie says.

Ah, they smile. They are Sylvia, Nora, Bibi, and Susan. Sylvia, the shortest, most talkative one, says, "We make our names easy for you." Then she announces, "I am the playmaker."

"You bring the ball down court," I say.

"Yes!"

"Who is the shooter? You?" I say to Susan beside me.

"They all score!" Sylvia laughs. "I feed them."

Unlike the Requalifiers or my Fourth Year students, they warm up fast. They are in high school in Ružomberok; they study English, economics, geography, literature; their basketball team is sponsored by a local club that sends them to Italy, Spain, Poland; they are a Junior team, but next year they can play Senior ball if they are good enough. Susan, they say, is good enough right now. In fact, she has played in several Senior games already. Sylvia proudly says that two years ago, at sixteen, Susan was recruited for Ružomberok, brought there from Stará Tura, given an apartment, money to live on. "Oh yes, Susan will be big!" Sylvia promises.

Susan is already at least six feet tall and, I'm guessing, not easily pushed around. Last week, Sylvia says, they were in Valencia. Susan's brother, a student there, came to watch them play. "Yes," Susan says, "maybe I will study in Valencia too, if I don't sign with a professional team."

"A professional team in Slovakia?" Lizzie asks.

Of course, they all say. In Ružomberok they draw 300 people a game! Better than Bratislava, where maybe only fifty come.

"Why is that?" I ask. "It's the capital."

They laugh. Maybe there is nothing else to do in Ružomberok! All four women are relaxed and at ease with us, confident. In Bratislava tomorrow they will play an exhibition game against an Austrian team, and they expect to win; afterwards they will enjoy a hot shower, a good meal, and maybe—why not?—some dancing. I am for them, with them, and though I can't watch them play tomorrow because I will be giving a poetry reading at Comenius University, I will be closer to them, I think, than to any of their countrymen.

I ask if the Czech-Slovak split will change things much for them. No, they shrug. I ask if it's better in Slovakia now than three years ago.

"Maybe," says Sylvia.

"Could you travel to Italy and Spain before the Revolution?"

"Me? I was too young. But my father—of course." Her father is the manager of their club. Before becoming manager, he too was an athlete and could travel anywhere. "But he is not a businessman," she wants to make clear. This is a delicate point, because "manager" in her part of the world now is a complex

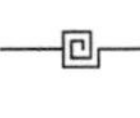

word: formerly it meant "important Party functionary"; now it describes, more often than not, a former Communist who emerged from the Revolution with money from a strong box or a secret Swiss bank account, money he could invest, hence a capitalist, a mover and shaker, perhaps a quick-change artist. (I think of Igor and his private bookshop.) But this is messy territory, nothing like a basketball court, where the lines are clearly drawn and everything is in the open, so we turn our attention to the window, and we're passing the town where the delicious Figaro chocolate is made—have we tried it?

Then we pass another town, where the players say a nuclear reactor sits, boiling away—"the dirtiest anywhere." We pass Stará Tura, where Susan grew up. All of these connections are suddenly bouncing around the compartment like so many loose basketballs: revolution, candy, poison, home. Talk about messy. Well, we don't. We change the subject, focus on Bratislava. We are all eager to arrive and be hosted, honored, distracted by the capital. And, for further consideration, Bratislava is only a short hop—or a good swim across the Danube—from Vienna, gateway to the fabulous West.

Yes, Slovakia is difficult to talk about, but so is a rainbow, so is a fish. Maybe that's why none of my colleagues at the university except for the Grmelas—who scarcely count because they are Czech and never joined the Party—have invited us into their homes. Things are too much right now—too hopeful, too slippery, too messy. Meeting at the police station is one thing; where one sleeps and perhaps dreams is another. They say, "We must get together and really talk—soon"—then look at their watches—"but not today, unfortunately"—and rush off to class. It is like a refrain, a tic, a speech for a play that doesn't have much development. But the locked-in is everywhere: from the glum silence on the city buses to—ironically—the best essay written in English (despite its content it won, I was told, because it had no grammatical errors and was therefore declared perfect) to my Fourth Year students who worry about their exams because they don't know *the* answer. When I handed out a list of questions at the start of the year and explained we would look for different ways to respond, they said, "But there is only one way." No ambiguity for them. A poem, a story, or a novel is not a work of imagination reflecting the richness and complexity of the human condition but a document of almost legal shape, a treatise, a blueprint demonstrating something black and something white, and it all means *this* . . . in a sentence or two.

"But why?" I burst out. "I mean, why *now?*" They gaze at their hands, are still.

I think of Luba Baranova's parting remark, "You know, we are used to behaving. Under the Nazis, under the Communists, we were good." I think of Katarina Fetkova, who chairs the English department at the University of Mateja Bela in Banská Bystrica, the school where Party members once went for seminars to keep rigid. She invited me there to give a poetry reading. "You will have an attentive audience. We are a rural people—like everywhere in Slovakia—trained not to make noise."

Later, she said, "Allow me to tell you a kind of fable. There are all these young children who receive very nice treatment, warm attention; even their schools seem cleaner and brighter than schools for older kids. As they grow up, less personal attention is paid to them, for they are being divided into two basic groups—the clever and the dull—and given their lessons in earnest. The clever will go to the university, the dull to trade school, but in either case they will want the same things. It is no accident," Katarina Fetkova said, "that we live as we do."

But once a beautiful moment: I said to my Fourth Year students, "You know, when I appear to be angry with you, I'm really not. I'm only pretending to be angry—it's a ruse, an attempt to get you to *talk*." A little voice among them said, "It's like us.

When we appear to be quiet, we're really not. We're only pretending to be quiet."

The train makes one more stop before Bratislava. The Madonna fan and her man depart, and we are joined by a woman wearing a squeaky-new leather jacket and carrying a big cardboard box that Sylvia helps her settle on the floor. The woman, about forty, is all smiles when she hears English being spoken. She tells Sylvia to tell us that she gets English on her TV every day now because she has a dish! We all acknowledge her good fortune.

Now she wants to open her box and show the Americans something. *Here! Look!* She takes out a handful of dolls—each maybe three inches tall—made from cornhusks. At first I think they are little girls wearing some kind of festive Slovak headwrap, but no, they are Jesus dolls, 200 of them, and the yellow headwrap is a halo. She, her husband, and their son spent all week constructing them. The son helped because he wishes to buy a motorcycle with his share, the mother says, smiling, proud of his ambition. Yes, she is taking the dolls to Bratislava for the tourists. Are we tourists?

Sylvia explains that I am a visiting professor at the university in Prešov, and the woman says, "*Ano, ano,*" and puts away her dolls.

I ask how long she has been making them. She holds up three fingers: three years. She is beaming. And every week she can travel to the city and trade them for designer jeans, leather jackets, a satellite dish, even a motorcycle! She sinks back in her seat. "Life," she sings in English, "is A-okay." I catch Sylvia's eye. She who has 300 Ružomberok fans come to watch her dribble a ball, she whose father manages a club that sponsors a team that can travel to Italy or Spain—that has been able to travel outside the country for years—she shrugs and gives me a grin that says, I think, *So what else is new?*

Recalling the Last Day

When we met Katarzyna in the High Tatras I did not think of Warsaw, her native city, but of Vienna. She would almost shine in Vienna, where so many shop windows glitter with riches and half of the city seems to have issued from luxury hotels or embassies or five-star restaurants to take the successful air of the place. Despite what she told us, that she had no more money and could finally *breathe,* I could see her sitting quite at home in an open horse cab wearing a hat and coat of matching fur—and then saying to her companion after he pointed out the prime minister and his wife strolling past St. Stephen's Cathedral, "Oh, really? But they look like everybody else." We in fact did see the PM and his wife out strolling one day; a local man named Ziggy, who had overheard us talking and wanted to show us around, indicated them to us: a handsome couple, and indeed they did blend into the whole—no one was making a fuss at their presence—but for that reason I think Katarzyna would be disappointed. High glamour was missing, not even an attending policeman, and they were on foot!

What would amuse her? The hotel where Mozart wrote "The Marriage of Figaro"? Where Freud lived? Schubert's birthplace? Look, imbedded into stone beside St. Stephen's main entrance there is an ancient circle, a measurement, which decreed the minimum size a loaf of bread could be. You could place your small loaf against the circle and expose your stingy baker to the world! "No, no, my angel," she would say to her companion, "none of these things amuses me now." But she *does* need to do something because she has had enough of this horse cab, you understand? She has given up roulette, given up blackjack—and thank God, too: the fortune she lost! not to mention almost her life!—but she has given up cigarettes, as well, and she would like something to do with her hands right now.

"Perhaps a coffee and cake aboard the *Johann Strauss?*" he suggests.

"Yes," she sighs, "that might be fun."

Katarzyna is a large-breasted big woman with flowing blonde hair. It is clear that in front of her mirror she takes her time. The day we met her she had already changed clothes three times and would change once more before the night was over. It was New Year's Eve. She and her companion Rudy and her son Franz had taken the train from Warsaw to Zakopane, and from there a hired taxi took them across the Slovak border and forty miles down to Tatranská Lomnica and the Grand Hotel Praha. She changed into a skiing costume because Rudy had produced cross-country skis; but this adventure did not prove satisfying—

she kept falling down. Rudy said, "Well, the trails are too slick today. Perhaps tomorrow there will be fresh snow." Franz, who was fifteen, was having a fine time on his skis, but Katarzyna declared she had had enough of this for one day so they all returned to the hotel to change clothes for a light supper, and then rest up for the gala, indeed historic, party the Praha was throwing that night. Lizzie and I met them at the light supper.

We were staying in Ždiar, a small folk village roughly halfway between Zakopane and Tatranská Lomnica, in the home of Pan a Pani Vojtasak. David and Sophie. They had three rooms upstairs that they rented out, rooms that David finished off in knotty pine and that Sophie furnished with thick down comforters sewn with her own hands; mornings a great white light entered the valley and bounced off the snow-covered hills across the road. We had the middle room, a Hungarian family on one side of us, a German family on the other. Lizzie and I never had a real conversation with either family, although we laughed a lot with the Germans in goofy pidgin while making popcorn and telling about our days: "Oh la-la" and "zoom!" They had two boys, aged nine and twelve, and all four were a sunny, peppy lot come there, as we all had, to ski. The Hungarians were dark and mostly silent, and in our communal kitchen they kept their foodstuffs and utensils clearly separate. They had a boy and girl about the same ages as the German kids, but the four youngsters never mixed that I could see. On Christmas morning Lizzie tried to tell the Hungarian father that we had enjoyed hearing—through the wall between us—the lovely flute music they had played the previous evening. Apparently understanding only the part about the music coming through the wall, he said, defensively, "Problem? Problem?"

We arrived in Ždiar two days before Christmas, taking the bus up from gray, gloomy Prešov with our bags and skis and, unknown to me, some tree decorations for which Lizzie had a plan. Our first day we walked through the village whose simple wooden houses went back to a time before Communism was even thought of, bought things to cook and drink, got giddy over a horse-drawn sleigh passing by, the horse dropping its steaming pucky in the road, the sun easing down behind the mountains turning the sky a plum color, ice forming in my beard. Beside the road the Biela River ran clear and sparkled in moonlight and even in those places where it ran under snow-covered ice we could still hear it, and we sang out, "Nothing like Prešov!" That night we raised our glasses to Nadia, who had asked Dada to find us a room, private rooms and hotels in that region being booked months in advance—a year in advance—and we hoped to see her soon. We also had Nadia to thank for our skis and boots. We had followed her one night to a cavernous warehouse somewhere under the university where one man produced what we wanted and another man, portly, obviously important judging from how Nadia and the first man kept smiles ready in case he looked at them, busied himself with an ink pen he needed to poise just so over the paper laid out for his signature. When he finished scratching his name he blew on the ink as if it—or his name—or both—were wonderful delicate creations, like parts of a soup, and he had not had a bite of anything all day! But eventually he turned the narrow Mongolian eyes in his fleshy face at smiling Nadia and allowed her to have the paper.

I think of Nadia now in Vienna. She has arrived for the day with her shopping bag containing the sandwiches she brought from Slovakia and which she will eat in a quiet place outdoors watching the lucky strollers who issue from this luxury hotel or that museum or that open horse cab. That's all she does here—look. I wonder what she and Katarzyna would say to each other if they were introduced, the one who can afford to come to

Vienna only for the day, and only if she brings her own food, the other who left her homeland twenty years ago and scooped up so much money at the gaming tables of Monte Carlo she would have died from it but for this angel you see beside her, this lovely man Rudy. Rudy smiles. Franz smiles too, in his necktie and blazer.

"Elegant, no?" Katarzyna says to us. "At his Swedish school he must dress like this, and why not? It is very exclusive, very expensive, and Franz loves it, don't you, darling?" Franz says, "I can speak five languages, so I guess it's a pretty good school." "You are like me," his mother says, "I pick up language like this!" and she snaps her fingers, makes that motion anyway, but there is no actual snap, only a *fip,* because of the long formal gloves she wears. She also wears a red low-cut evening gown showing her creamy shoulders and decides we must have wine—yes, Rudy?—for the party is about to begin! We drink a toast with these three travelers from Warsaw about whom we know almost nothing yet except that they have come to the High Tatras to be amused (the Czechs and Slovaks are breaking up at midnight, are they not? a divorce like this does not happen every day)—and we have joined their table at the Grand Hotel Praha's New Year's Eve party in our hiking boots and jeans because earlier we'd stopped at the hotel for something to eat to warm us up for the trip back to Ždiar and heard this very American voice at the next table offer to gloss the menu for us. The voice belonged to Rudy.

"There's not much," he said. "The cabbage soup is okay. I understand they're saving the good stuff for the party."

"Are you coming?" the woman beside him suddenly asked us.

"We didn't know about it."

"There will be two empty chairs at our table," she said.

"Sure," Rudy said, "think about it."

So we stayed because we had spent eight days in storybook Ždiar skiing and hiking and that morning decided to spend New Year's Eve poking around somewhere else. We rode the bus over to Starý Smokovec, which is the oldest resort in the High Tatras, and bought postcards, window shopped, had fun doing nothing really, and then went up to The Grand Hotel (1904) for roast trout served to us by waiters in tuxedos in an elegant room. Over our wine we got an idea. After this, why not walk the six or seven kilometers up to Tatranská Lomnica—which was on the way back to Ždiar—and have dinner at *its* Grand Hotel? Lunch and dinner in Grand Hotels back to back on New Year's Eve! On Czechoslovakia's last day! Why indeed not! Outside, big fat snowflakes were floating down in our faces, and Lizzie said, "We're inside one of those glass bowls you shake up. Hang on, Doctor!"

Halfway to Tatranská Lomnica we noticed a very handsome hotel-looking building whose sign said ŠKOLA. It didn't look like any school we had seen in Slovakia; there were tiers of private balconies for sitting out in the sun or under the stars, an overall shine to the place. A woman carrying skis came along, rosy-cheeked, athletic, clearly refreshed from her day on the slopes, and we spoke, introduced ourselves, said we were curious about this beautiful school that looked like, well, a posh hotel. "Ah," she said, beaming, gazing at it. When her small son Marek came rushing up to hug her knees, she said, "I have a nice Moravian vodka inside—and cookies for Marek—would you like to sit?"

We followed them into the bright, clean building, passed several bulletin boards with children's bright drawings on them, and went up to her room. Her name was Zuzana. She used to be with the Education Ministry, she told us, but three years ago there were "many changes" (she scowled—clearly revolution wasn't her cup), and so now she taught at the Teachers College in Bratislava. For years she and other members of the Ministry and their children had had use of the škola for their winter holidays, though after this winter, she sighed, it was doubtful that they could return. Her eyes followed Marek's hand as he drew blue crayon circles on a piece of paper. "Faces," she smiled at us. Then, "The school is for sick children who come here to breathe, from all over, even Africa, and don't you think it's beautiful?" Again we said we did. I also thought of Nadia; she too had been a member of the Party. It was remarkable how much these women—especially in the eyes—seemed to resemble each other.

Katarzyna's eyes, however, glitter. I am sure they glittered even on the sleeper that she and Rudy and Franz brought down from Warsaw under the Polish stars. She too is a star, flecks of silver and gold appear on her eyelids, on a plum-colored background reminding me of night coming down over Ždiar, applied with a brush, with the hand of an artist. "I must write my life story," she announces, "it will make a fantastic movie. Fantastic!" And she smoothes out the long white formal gloves she wears, admiring the fit around her fingers, the diamonds sparkling at her wrist, her bare upper arms and shoulders, her ample breasts and red gown—all of it—admiring all of it as if in this brilliant moment the cameras are actually rolling. Franz says, "Red and white are the colors of Poland." But Katarzyna doesn't hear him, or chooses not to. And why should she? Poland is only a country; she resides in the heavens. At the light supper two hours before when we first met and she was all in black, tight-fitting sleek black from neck to knees, her hat, also black, circled out, out, like the rings around a planet, and when she held her head just so, one glittering eye peeked out from under the brim like the first star of evening. And now behold her, perhaps an entire galaxy.

"Well," Lizzie says, "don't you all look nice."

"Oh, it's just something I put on for tonight," Katarzyna says.

Her men bow in their dark jackets; there is a light sky-blue tie on Franz, a deep red one on Rudy: nice complements to the lady.

"I come from Minnesota," Rudy says. "Educated in St. Paul. For the past two years I've been living in Warsaw."

"This makes me very happy," Katarzyna says. "And you?" she asks us.

"Wait," Rudy says. "May I guess? Your accents are Midwest. I'd say Illinois."

"Very close," Lizzie says. "Iowa."

"Actually," he says, "I *was* going to say western Illinois. Dialect is a small hobby of mine."

"Angel, please, may I interrupt? I know these waiters, and I know we should order as soon as possible. We must have wine—yes, Rudy? And lots of water. Once the party begins we will never see them."

A ticket to the party costs 600 crowns. This gives you a dinner of caviar egg with ham, beefsteak Carmen, potatoes, rice, and vodka. The ticket also allows you to choose from a lavish buffet laid out with suckling pig, beef, fowl, fish, cakes, sweets designed like little castles, salads, fruits, compotes, on and on, and for these things you pay extra. But the basic ticket—or 1,200 crowns for two—represents one-third of Nadia's monthly salary at the university. At the current rate of exchange 1,200 crowns is about $40. Katarzyna has suggested that Rudy order two bottles of wine, one red, one white, two bottles of Russian champagne ("It's the best, of course!"), five bottles of mineral water, a liter of orange juice, and a couple of Pepsis. Rudy gets all this done, in Polish, and Katarzyna says to him, "*Dobrze, dobrze.*" Good, good. Soon she will say much more; she is eager to talk, to produce verbal glittering snapshots, ritzy details, all focused on money and glamour and intrigue; the Mafia is involved too, oh yes, and how she paid them back, every cent, and how she lost her film business in Warsaw, how she had left

Poland twenty years ago and returned three years ago to sell, sell, and then took that money and threw it all away at roulette, blackjack ("Quick, quick, I wanted quick results, everything on one card, one little bounce!"), but oddly nothing about the recent great political changes, the fall of Communism, and very little about Rudy except that he was the angel who saved her. Yes, who *is* this angel from Minnesota? "Actually, I speak nine languages," he says after ordering, "and you'd think Polish would be easy for me. But it's not." The wine arrives quickly. We raise our glasses, a clarinet is squealing in the background.

On Christmas Eve, our first full day of skiing in Ždiar, we found a trail that ran beside the Biela River and then cut up into the hills following another stream. It went up and up and often we stopped to catch our breath or to admire the icy stream, the surprising patterns it made, the silvery skyscapes and rugged faces; all around us it was wonderfully quiet except for the rushing water and some wind in the pines, and then we came to a great wide meadow with a small barn in the middle of it. A trough built around three sides of the barn was full of hay, and lining the meadow were trails made by animals that came down from the timber to feed there.

"Do you know what this *is,* Gary?"

We sat beside the barn feeling lucky and ate our apples and bread and imagined the meadow with animals on it in the moonlight; and then off a ways we saw a small wooden shed almost hidden by trees and a snowdrift. We went over to it. It was an observation post. In an hour or so it would be dusk and we could be in there, watching. We thought about it. We really wanted to do it. But we'd have to spend the night in the shed because we couldn't ski back in the dark, the going was mostly downhill and in places steep and too close to the icy stream; and if we stayed the night we'd have to give up Midnight Mass in

Ždiar. We wanted to do both. We fell back in the snow and made angels in all that quiet space.

"A manger," Lizzie whispered, as if she still could not believe our luck.

Eight days later I keep wanting to stop Katarzyna to ask about the spaces between the glittering snapshots, because I am more interested in what she isn't telling than the piles of chips she is scooping up. "I was rich, so rich you can't imagine, but a woman without a country. I am Polish of course but nowhere does it say that. My passport says Swedish. Impossible! Like my life. Which I must write down, yes? I play number 6, it wins, number 3, it wins. Who is this woman? Everyone wants to know."

In the light-hearted spirit of the party I ask her, "Yes, how *does* it happen that you carry this impossible Swedish passport?"

She looks at me. "I could tell you stories," she finally says. "Oh, yes."

"I'm listening."

"Well, for example, Franz' father. He marries this Swedish woman—does he know her?—and now he has a Swedish passport. But he is a Pole!"

"Excuse me," Franz says, "what was that? My father married a Swedish woman?"

She looks at him. "Yes, of course."

Franz says, "I don't believe it. He's never told me—"

"It's true, darling."

"What was her name?"

The mother sighs. "I don't remember."

Rudy puts a hand on the boy's shoulder, says something I don't catch, something soothing, manly, because Franz finally smiles and shrugs as if his mother's revelation is not so important.

He likes Rudy. Katarzyna likes Rudy too because he has just smoothed over an awkward moment—I can imagine he has done this before—and of course she likes him because he has rescued her. We don't know how exactly; Katarzyna hasn't gotten to that part yet, she is still winning money hand over fist, in Monte Carlo, in Spain, in Poland, too, it seems, although one day the Mafia comes along.

"They watch me, you see, winning all this money. Oh, once in a while I lose and have to go back to my hotel for more, and it's here, like silk, I am approached, when I am going out for more. Why trouble yourself? they ask. We know you are lucky. We will lend you money here, in the casino, and save you time. So I take their money. I run up a tab, is that right, Rudy? A tab?" Rudy nods. Katarzyna smiles. "You see why I must write my life story?"

Not exactly, I think. Not yet, anyway. What about Poland? What about the thugs running things there? But I hold my tongue. I don't want another awkward moment in front of Franz, who is a nice boy. Who has spent his life so far being a nice boy.

We left the barn in the meadow and skied back to Pan a Pani Vojtasak's house watching the sun leave the valley. On the way we broke off a pine bough. In our room Lizzie found a vase for it and put it in a window beyond which stars had come out. Three fat Slovak bulbs hung on the bough and wrapped presents lay underneath it when she was finished. We had spaghetti and lentils and red wine and a real Christmas tree—and candles—and this lovely flute music coming through the wall from the Hungarian side, and when the horse and sleigh went by in the road we heard those tiny bells.

Next morning Dada knocked at our door before breakfast and announced that Nadia had arrived to visit her in the neighboring valley, could we join them? Dada and her husband had a house over there; she fired directions—only a kilometer away, an easy walk for us, tomorrow, yes? Ski, eat something, and comes the darkness, it's okay, her husband has a car for the journey home.

We went. We were glad to see Nadia and to hear she was feeling better (earlier, in Prešov, her ulcers had been acting up). She produced a big box of cookies she had baked and Dada made coffee. Their husbands appeared: Dada's William, the ousted dean of ideology, and Nadia's Tibor, whom we'd heard had left Nadia for a younger woman but who had recently come back to her. We had been curious to see what these men looked like, and it turned out they looked like a lot of men who are fit and eat well and enjoy a robust joke and wish to continue this way of life. William and Tibor also might have been twin brothers. Not having much English they carried on a laughing conversation of their own, and Dada said to us, "Please, understand, they are laughing not at you, only at men they know—they like to—what is the word, Nadia?" "Mimic," Nadia said. "Yes, they like to mimic at them," Dada said. Nadia said she was dying for a cigarette and the others, all non-smokers, shouted, "No! Ski!"

The former dean of ideology led us out and stayed in the lead all day. More than once Dada said, "My husband is a *fanatic* for skiing!" Each time Nadia laughed, and finally Dada said, "This is not a good word?" Yes, it was perfect, Nadia assured her. We skied around the rim of the valley called Bachledova; it was more open than the Ždiar valley, you could see great and beautiful distances, and Nadia said to us, "I could never afford to come here if Dada did not invite me. I am always happy to accept. I feel free." We looked at the long valley running below and in the distance the white hills repeating themselves and the mountain beyond, and I remembered her comment after we left the cavernous room in Prešov with our skis: "You will be happy in Ždiar. You will have the two most important things—snow and a warm woman."

Back at the former dean's house he opened two bottles of beer, which we all shared, and Nadia passed her box of cookies. "So. Tell us how you are enjoying yourselves among the folk," she said. We told about finding the manger on Christmas Eve and attending Midnight Mass and how wonderfully quiet it was in the hills and how refreshing all this was after Prešov, after even Vienna; especially after Vienna, we said. "Oh, really?" Nadia said. "Even after Vienna? Surely you don't mean it." We did mean it and tried to explain about the glitter, and Dada said, "No, no, you are having a joke." So we tried to change the subject, but Nadia wanted us to know what it was like when she went to Vienna, carrying her shopping bag, her food, too poor to afford the prices there. "You understand?"

It was getting dark. The dean took an old hatchet off the wall and showed it to me. "Peasants," he smiled. "He means peasants used that ax many years ago," Nadia explained. He and Tibor laughed. Then the dean said to me, "But you, in my opinion, you are Paul Bonyan!" He thought this was enormously funny. So did his twin. I might have thought it was funny too, but I was hungry now, getting a headache, and no one was saying anything about eating, although Nadia kept urging more cookies on us. Finally Lizzie and I said we had better go, it was getting late. "Yes," Dada said, "you must be tired." She said nothing about her husband's car, which was fine, we just wanted to leave.

Katarzyna has won half a million dollars and lost it. She sold her film business in Warsaw and lost that money too. She couldn't stop gambling until the money was all gone. "I had a sickness," she says, slowly peeling off a long white glove. "I needed a thrill, that high you feel just before the little ball stops bouncing, just before the final card is exposed. I needed people to applaud my daring. But that"—the glove completely off now—"is all finished. I am cured. I am poor and happy and lovely Rudy understands this. He is such an angel, you can't imagine." She gives him her bare hand to hold. "You see, I thought I could continue winning forever! And why not? Look at this fantastic luck I have in the beginning, at Monte Carlo, number 6, number 3, and every time my number comes up! That's where my story begins—and where the movie should begin too, don't you think?"

She looks at me to say something, and I say, "Why not?"

Rudy says, "Yes, the key was understanding her feeling of inferiority. Once we got that out, the rest was relatively easy."

So that's what Rudy is, I'm thinking, a shrink. Of course. I watch him press her hand between his palms.

They gaze at each other, and he says, "A great success."

She whispers, "Thank you, my sweet."

"Oh no, it is I who thanks *you*."

"This hand you are holding is free," she says. "Free of my sickness."

"Katarzyna is a brave woman," he says.

She lowers her eyes a moment, then gives the rest of us a big smile. A smile that, surely, must be included in the movie of her life.

Rudy picks up his glass. "A toast," he says, "to survival!" We all drink. We are all part of this movie now, are we not? (If in fact we haven't always been part of it, for better or for worse.) Come richly together to celebrate bravery, escape, success, history, romance, you name it. And this Russian champagne *is* good and I am happy to have Katarzyna refill my glass.

"So tell me, George," she says. "How old are you and what brings you to Slovakia?"

"No, no, don't tell her," Franz says, "let me guess. You're forty-six."

"I was forty-six eight years ago," I tell him, "thanks." Then to his mother: "I lived in Warsaw before the revolution and wanted to come back to eastern Europe to see how things are going. Also, my grandfather was born just over the mountains—in a Polish village called Ostrów. I'd like to see it."

"That is poor land in that part of Poland," she says, and resumes an intimacy with her glass.

"Well, well," says Rudy. "I have Polish roots too. Same connection, my grandfather, and in many ways that's why I took a job in Warsaw." He raises his glass to me, "*Na zdrowie!*"

We drink to our Polish grandfathers.

"So what's it like," I say, "practicing psychiatry in Warsaw?"

"Psychiatry?"

"Aren't you a shrink?"

"No, no," he laughs, "I'm a banker."

The lights—a magnificence of them—suddenly come on in the ceiling of the Grand Hotel Praha's central room, where the musicians have assembled to help us keep time at this historic dance, and where the grand old mirrors all around allow Katarzyna to look up and see, at any moment, how we, and she, in the wavy reflection, are doing. This is her element as truly as water is for a fish, indeed she is almost floating in the chandelier's shimmering light, floating and bouncing at the same time if that is possible, and of course it is! Anything and everything is possible! You can even lose and win simultaneously, no? "Yes, I am poor as a church mouse," our beauty says, "but I am on fire with happiness." Nadia says, "When I am in Vienna, sitting on my bench, I can tell you exactly who lives there and who does not, from the shopping bags they carry." Rudy says, "I have lived in nine countries abroad and except for Poland I've picked up the local language within six months. I think Katarzyna has made me lazy." "But I am worth it, my angel, am I not?" "Yes," he says, "I'm not even running as much as I used to. I'd get up at five o'clock and put in ten miles almost every day—at least ten miles. But now," he smiles at her, "look at me." "I am looking, my angel." "And if they don't carry a shopping bag," Nadia says, "I can tell from the look in their eyes. It's just like mine."

Only a prying bore would ask Katarzyna about the spaces, the distances, between the glittering snapshots. Only a wise guy would want to know how she gets from here to there while keeping her hair so neatly in place. I did say though, thanks to that excellent champagne, "Well, since you asked me, let me ask how old *you* are."

She looks at her son, then at Rudy, and finally at me and says, "Forty-six." That popular number seems about right, and I nod, and for an instant I think she wants to hit me. But she cuts her eyes to Lizzie, "And you, ah—"

"Elizabeth," Franz helps her.

"Yes, of course," she says. "How old are *you*, Elizabeth?"

Lizzie tells her—thirty-eight—and then Katarzyna says to Rudy, "I would like to dance now."

It is so cold walking to Midnight Mass that the snow squeaks when we step on it. To our left the dark hills and the dark mountain beyond them are one and where the mountain stops the toss of brilliant stars begins, and down close beside us we can see the icy Biela River in the moonlight and hear it moving. All of this I think as we walk in the squeaky snow is a perfect illustration of where everything should be. We make out other walkers on the road, at first only a couple here, a couple there, old women arm in arm, we see, as we pass them: small women in big boots and babushkas huddled down against themselves and against the cold. As we approach the center of the village, more huddled shapes come into the road, old and young, dozens of them now, and all of us ascending the hill among murmurs of greeting, the smoke of our breath, to the white building where they are singing.

Inside it's packed near the entrance and I think we'll have to stand, but then I remember how it is on the buses in Slovakia—if people get inside the door, somehow that's good enough—so I ease through this crowd, pulling Lizzie with me, and sure enough, way up front there is a pew for us. The singing has stopped and now a communal saying of the rosary begins. We can see our breath, see everyone's breath. We can also see, flanking the altar, two scrawny pine trees strung with lights that blink on and off like displays in a department store, red, yellow, blue they blink, according to a fixed pattern, making everything around the altar look cheap and gaudy, 1950s dime store, basement rec room in the American suburbs. Put a couple of bubbling beer displays up there and they'd look right at home. It occurs to me that the trees are almost without needles by design, to better show off the precision of the blinking pattern. But the Slovaks must think the lights are beautiful, a release into glory after years of darkness.

I should leave. I'm too angry to be there. When the acolyte comes out to light the candles I want him to light hundreds, thousands, not stop at a puny six; I want warmth, real fire, at least the smell of wax—beeswax, tallow, a melting down, joinery; I want to make a speech to the congregation: those goddamn blinking lights don't belong in here!

But I stay, of course, and something happens, something I have never seen before: at Communion time the men go up first, beginning with the oldest grandfather and ending with the smallest boy, one long line representing perhaps the span of a century, white-bearded at the front, pink-faced at the back; and then after the last boy, standing right behind him, is an old woman not much taller than he is who may be well over a hundred and is assisted as she hobbles up the aisle by hands reaching out from the pews along the way, and walking behind her are Ždiar's other old women who one by one become younger as they approach the priest. No one that I can see has arranged this order; it has been devised by the villagers themselves on the spot and without discussion, and whatever it means, if it means anything at all beyond a vivid ordering of time, it seems as powerful as the light which will rise in the east tomorrow, to give us what it gives. The blinking lights are gone. They have slipped away, and I do not think about them until a week later when we all rise to watch a clock hung with balloons—and when a fading Polish beauty will ask for two 500 crown notes from her banker, one to tuck in her son's blazer pocket, the other between her breasts. "If you do this on New Year's Eve, on the stroke of midnight," she says, "you will never be poor." Then she laughs—at the ritual? herself?—holding nothing back. And still laughing she embraces her angel, waiting for the proper moment to kiss him.

Where To?

On the bus that would take us into Poland there were five other passengers and all of them were smugglers. They had come down to Slovakia early that morning, loaded up with vodka and hair coloring in Prešov, and now as we rode north four of them were busy working on ways to hide the stuff, to avoid paying the Polish import tax. Lizzie and I watched them.

The one who wasn't fussing was feeling good. He stood in the aisle combing his black cowlick and sang a song about swans. The young woman who resembled Ingrid Bergman fixed a pillow under her sweater to look pregnant, then got out knitting needles and a partially finished rug; she spread her knitting over the sackful of hair coloring boxes in the seat beside her, a wary expression in her gray eyes but otherwise the picture of serene budding motherhood.

The other three Poles were jittery as squirrels. The thin one had packaged his hair coloring in a crate that resembled an air-conditioning unit and placed it under a rear seat. He sat near the front and every time the bus bumped or turned sharply in the twisty road he would hustle back to check on the crate, nudge it with his foot to line it up just so.

The heavy woman in the first seat, catty-corner from the driver, had both vodka and hair dye. She spent much of the journey to the border telling the driver how good the hair coloring was, holding up a box for him to see. Look, she said, very beautiful red tint, very natural—and such a good price! She regretted now the vodka, it took up too much room, she should have stayed with the hair coloring. Look, she said to the driver, didn't he agree it was beautiful? He said, "*Tak, tak,*" yes, yes, but kept his eyes on the road. She had her vodka in a large suitcase and the hair coloring in two duffel bags piled on top of it, everything snug in the seat beside her, patting the arrangement and cooing as if she had a pet in there that needed comforting.

Finally, the man with the mustache—the least organized of all—who stood in the aisle as if in despair over his two jumbo suitcases of vodka that took up two seats. An hour out of Prešov he was still debating whether to leave them as they were or try to push them under the seats. Too full, too full, he kept telling the man who was feeling good. His eyes drooped like a basset hound's.

Back in Prešov he'd helped me out. I approached the driver to buy my tickets.

"*Dokąd?*" the driver said. Where to?

"Krosno," I said.

He told me how much in złotys. I offered him crowns.

"Polish bus, Polish money," he said.

I didn't have any.

He shrugged. "*Szkoda.*" Too bad.

I knew what the exchange rate was, more or less, and offered extra crowns. He shook his head; he couldn't be bothered. He was waiting, I reckoned, for dollars. I was about to pull some out when the man with the mustache said, "Here." He handed me 100,000 złotys. "Give me two hundred crowns." I was happy to let him make a good commission so I could save my dollars for Poland.

On the bus, he asked if I would carry two of his bottles across the border. I said sure. Why were we going to Krosno? he asked. I explained we were going beyond it, to Rzeszów, spending the night, then going to a small village, Ostrów, where my *dziadek,* Stefan Szostak, was born.

The man who was feeling good had joined us. When he heard I was a Polish grandson he immediately brought me a plastic glass filled with vokda and orange pop. He was Marek, he said. We told him our names. He said, "No Gary, no Elizabeth. Gariego, Elzbieta." Then—beaming—"Chicago!"

We told him no, Iowa. But next year Idaho.

"Idaho? Idaho? *Dlaczego?*" Why?

For the mountains, we told him.

Ah, he smiled. "*Tak, tak,*" and said Elzbieta needed vodka. I told him no, only me, and put my hand on Lizzie's stomach. *Dziecko,* child.

He slapped me on the back. "A child! Okay!" And insisted we toast the child, Elzbieta, grandfather Szostak, Chicago, the mountains, the U.S.A., Poland, and finally this good Polish bus. "Not bad," he said, "is life."

The man with the mustache, who had eased away during all this, now returned. He had two more bottles he wished for me to carry over the border. "You can do it, no problem." I said okay. Then he showed me a bus ticket to Rzeszów, saying I would need 40,000 złotys for it. I counted out enough crowns to trade, plus a tip. He shook his head sadly; he had no more złotys. I handed back the two bottles. He looked shocked. Marek roared, then said, "Greedy boy." He waved Mustache away and produced the złotys I needed.

As the bus slowed for the border crossing, the driver barked, "*Pivo! Pivo!*" Marek got two bottles of Czech pilsner from his bag and handed them up. When the Polish guard came to the driver's window, the bottles were stealthily slipped out. Then we waited while he returned to his shed; the five smugglers sat up straight and kept their eyes dead ahead, as if to show how good they could be. He came back with a clipboard and directed the driver to step out and open the storage area. He did. Then the guard boarded the bus.

He walked slowly to the rear, saying nothing. The heavy woman looked in a small mirror and put on fresh lipstick, watching him; as he passed, the knitter belched, patting her stomach, clacking her needles; the thin man bent to tie his shoelace and looked back along the aisle to see how his fake air-conditioner would fare; Marek produced a small black book and a thoughtful expression; Mustache sat with his feet on the two jumbo suitcases that he'd finally decided to push to the floor. The guard only glanced at us. He finished his stroll and waved us on. After the driver crossed into Poland, just out of sight of the border station, he pulled over, and the smugglers scrambled out as if the bus were on fire. Cigarettes were lit and glasses filled. By God, they'd done it! For only two bottles of Czech beer and a presentation of respect!

The next day a bus delivered Lizzie and me to a country crossroads. "Ostrów," the driver said. In a circle of speckled shade made by a single oak, a dozen mares and colts stood muzzle to muzzle while a man measured bellies, examined teeth.

Other men watched. Judging from the shapes of jaws and noses and full, unbroken eyebrows, I reckoned they were all kin to me. They took us in, briefly, shyly. A breeze came and pushed over green hay in the field beside us, and then the grass sprung up straight again. Time present and time past seemed one time and unconcerned with itself. I could have hung around that single tree for as long as I did my grandfather's orchard and creek and forge, simply waiting for the next thing, but after a while we walked up the country road in the spring air toward a lone house.

It was a café. We ate bean soup and bread. I asked the teenaged girl serving us if any Szostaks lived in Ostrów. She shrugged. Then, leading us outside, she pointed to a wooden steeple rising above a cluster of trees down the road. The village center. I asked about a *cmentarz.* She said, "*Tak,*" and pointed to a rise just up the road.

We started for the cemetery. Lizzie sighed when a stork flew directly over us, flapping and clacking stork-talk, she said. "I'm sorry, Dr. G., it's almost too damn much." Beans and wheat grew in fields on either side of us, and in the distance, across from the cemetery, a white horse, a plow, and a man—the reins looped around his neck—cut fresh furrows, like waves, in a soft, brown, almost perfectly round hill.

The treeless graveyard seemed far too big, too populous, for such a small village. Months before, in a reference book on patronymic surnames, I found Szostak and Szostek, good Polish names. I also found Shostack, Shustak, Shustek, Shostag (East German), and Šesták (Czech). All were derived, the book said, from Belorussian Shostakovich. There was conjecture that the names were connected to the word *shast,* six, possibly denoting a person with six fingers on one hand. In the Ostrów cemetery I seemed to have extra fingers on both hands, but still was finding no Szostaks or anything close. When I looked up to stretch my back, the farmer and his beautiful white horse continued to cut their wavelike furrows in the brown hill. I wanted to go ask him his name, and his horse's. Then Lizzie, in a far row, said she'd found one. Maria Szostak Something, who died in 1933 or 1938. We found more, pressing our fingers against the fading letters and numbers as if tracing them into the soft stone.

The village center consisted of a simple, bark-colored old wooden church, several shade trees, and a packed-dirt area where horse carts could park. We approached a man lying in his empty grain cart under a tree, having a smoke. Waving my arm around, I asked, "Szostak?" He sat up, looked at the sky, then smiled and pointed down a lane to a barn. There, Lizzie and I found a pink-cheeked old man searching his tool bench. I asked him, "Szostak?" He glanced at our bags twice, then took off on a hard dirt path.

"Are we supposed to follow him?" Lizzie said.

"I think so."

We met a man on a bicycle, at whom our guide fired some Polish. The man got off his bike, let it fall; now the two of them led us. We came to a stream and walked beside it. We were in a forest, though here and there, as if part of the natural setting, a weathered house abruptly revealed itself. I thought of the Gypsy settlement below Šariš Castle. Our guides stopped at a little house held up, it appeared, by cherry and apple trees. The cyclist knocked on the door; a man came out and said he was Andrzej, grandson of Maria Szostak. He looked so much like my uncle Joe I had trouble making verbs, the possessive. Reduced to nouns and pointing, I got across that I too was the grandson of a Szostak.

"Moment." He went back in and returned with a handsome carved chair, one clearly intended for special occasions. He set it under a cherry tree for Lizzie. He then brought out three more almost just like it: one for me, one for himself, and one that our two guides shared by sitting sideways with their elbows on their knees. Then Andrzej and I, using American place names and mainly Polish nouns (my plunge into pidgin had infected him), struggled and thought and slapped our foreheads and clapped our hands. "Moment!" He brought from the house an envelope, very old, bearing a Chicago return address. Everyone studied the writing, the stamps. Stamps licked by great-uncle Jakob—brother of Maria and Stefan! The bicyclist grabbed the sides of his head and exclaimed, in English, "Fantastic!" Andrzej gazed into the canopy of apple and cherry limbs shading us and could not stop smiling.

That night Lizzie and I stayed in the Hotel Cukrownia—the Hotel Sugar—which sat beside a sugar-beet factory five kilometers from Ostrów. It was a workers' hotel. We paid 110,000 złotys, about six dollars. I recorded this fact in my notebook, along with the detail that next door to our room a worker fried eggs in a communal kitchen for his dinner.

I thought about facts and details, about collecting them like eggs. About walking in the village that my grandfather walked away from and if our acts were facts. They didn't seem like facts; they seemed like something considerably less fixed for which I ought to have a good word.

I couldn't remember asking my mother very much about Grandpa when I was growing up. Not that I wasn't curious about him; but almost always there seemed to be this response in my family when I asked a question: "Just watch—and see." I was instructed by people who used their hands, who laid down a level and followed the bubble, who wiped a knife blade in the up position, not the down—so you won't hurt yourself, see? But once I heard words that were better than usual—words that didn't end when my mother stopped saying them. "He came from the Old Country, a handsome, educated young man—oh yes, very smart—and strong as a bull—he had to be, because of all the troubles he went through. They were always fighting over there, those Polish kings, those Russian Cossacks. On horses, with swords!" I had seen Grandpa drape complicated harnesses on his big-shouldered Belgians, seen him lift red-tipped pokers from the fiery forge, and I believed everything she told me. I still believed her, collecting my facts.

I knew the dangers of facts, their bullheaded insistence on making a straight line, a balanced weight, an answer the teacher will give you a star for and that you can tuck away in the place where you store your answers and stars. And maybe forget about. I did not want that. I did not want the exact number of clacking bones in a skeleton—I wanted what Joseph Conrad wanted, the questions, the mysteries, the imperfections and contradictions of the human heart. "A man's real life," he wrote, "is that accorded to him in the thoughts of other men by reason of respect or natural love." I respected my grandfather, but did I love him? Or did I love those images of him sending up sparks in his blacksmith shop, gazing at the sky in his bee-sweetened orchard, opening his book in the honeyed glow of a kerosene lamp at a table we all moved away from? "The dead," Conrad said, "can live only with the exact intensity and quality of life imparted to them by the living."

My mother was old enough to remember the day he came home from Ford's foundry, splashed on by molten steel. What a leap—from Polish kings to Detroit—and then another leap to a farm up north. The summers I was eight, nine, and ten, I followed him around. But the summer I turned eleven I elected to stay in Flint and play baseball. That August he died and was buried on my birthday. Almost two decades later Grandma, out of the blue, told me, "Korzeniowski, always reading this Korzeniowski, even on his last day." Trembling, I asked if I could see that last book. She said no, I couldn't, that it was gone.

All those years Steve Szostak had read Joseph Conrad, in Polish—even on his last day. But how would I know something like that? I knew other things. That he stood in a black rain and raised his fist at the heavens for drowning his beans. That he sat me on the hay wagon, between his knees, and gave me the reins to hold. Up and down the field we raced until Grandma came rushing out, her fist, her skirts, and the Polish flying, afraid I would be hurt. "He called her Nelly," my aunt Rita said, "did you know that?" I didn't. But I knew he had a mare named Nelly, and waded into the creek with her, and took off his shirt beside her, and bathed his scarred shoulders and back while she waited. In a photograph in my mother's house, Grandma wears a rose in her hair. She is sixteen, looking out at the world like a young woman who has spent the afternoon in her flower garden, alone, thinking how lovely everything is, how temporary, and just at that moment when happiness and melancholy compete most for her heart, the photographer snaps her. And later, in his studio, applies to her full and youthful cheeks a subtle blush.

In the Hotel Sugar, I stood at the window seeing stars, their random toss. I also saw a circle of sun-freckled farmers, a plowman and his beautiful white horse cutting wave-like furrows in a round hill. A stork flew over our heads, speaking to us. "How do you feel?" I said. "Everywhere," Lizzie said. We sat in special chairs under apple and cherry trees planted by a man with whom I shared a name we found fading on some stones. He couldn't stop shaking his head in wonder. I wondered, before we went away from those trees making speckled shadows in my wife's hair, if I would ever again see such bright shade. We had spent only a short while there, a blink in time; it was enough and not nearly enough.

Bringing Home the Baby

Earlier that spring, just before the trip to Ostrów, Lizzie boarded a plane in Košice and flew to Des Moines. Her father was in the hospital with his second heart attack—his first was three years before—and her mother had sent a telegram saying his chances this time appeared very slim. When Lizzie arrived at his bedside, she found him sitting up, telling jokes, asking for his pants. He was, the doctor said, a lucky man.

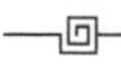

But Lizzie was feeling funny, swirly. A large thought occurred to her, even though she wasn't *that* late. She bought a take-home test at the drugstore, then saw an obstetrician. Bursting to tell me the results—in person—she flew back to Europe.

"Yes, yes—go," the doctor had said, "after all, you're only pregnant." Only? My god, she thought, why is this happening now?

She landed in Budapest, where I was waiting for her. She didn't tell me right away, and then not exactly. First she told me how her father was ("No more martinis!"), how my daughter Gretchen was ("Sailing through her last semester, planning to get an M.A. next, blooming!"), how my grandchildren Gabriel and Joanna were ("Taller, glowing!"), how a dozen other people back in the States were, how the weather was there, the food on the flight. By this time we were walking along the Danube, passing statues of kings looking stiff on their thrones. In my arms I carried apples and plums. Her eyes were luminous. "There's one more thing."

Six months later, in October, in Grangeville, Idaho, we were buying fruit trees from Rickman's nursery: a Toka, a Stanley, a Jonathan, a Gala. Alice Rickman, handing Lizzie her old Manx No Problem to hold, helped me load our trees into the pickup.

"What a day," Alice smiled. Everywhere you looked she had things breathing, lifting up, flicking out little jabs and nods at the autumn sun. Fine, filigreed wings of water from her sprinklers went *wish* and then *wish* over our shoulders. "Remember," she said, "trees appreciate some freedom. Above all, they favor a nice mucky soup to start out from." Lizzie handed back No Problem, a cat that possessed fresh bumps, a boxer's pushed-in aspect, and tender need. I thought he looked Irish, like my old friend Red Shuttleworth throwing his son batting practice on the Nebraska prairie.

We drove home. Up the mountain past Fred and Debbie Smith's MULE CROSSING sign, past Dave and Karen Bailey's grazing mares, past a blackberry patch that bears were already leaving their big seeded mushy pies in. Up and up. Hauling an orchard for the kid Lizzie and I started back in Slovakia, in a boxy prefab Socialist high-rise complete with a crumbling bunker, the principal view beyond our window cement. I was fifty-five, a grandfather, Lizzie thirty-nine. I was mumbling.

"Hold on," she said, "slow down and tell how I said get ready for a big surprise."

"You said it," I said, and commenced to dig three holes in the slope that our cat, Oshkosh, plucked mice from—plus a fourth hole under the bedroom window the kid could lean out and breathe in wafts of blossoming, hear the honeyed buzz of sweet dustings, the juicy enterprise.

All day I dug, separating rock and old root and some antlered bone from their deep suck. Two apple, two plum.

"That's four bases," I said, "a home run."

"Tell how Alice said deer, come snow, will covet your tender bark. That's a good line, it fits you," Lizzie said.

"Not right now. Right now," I said, "I want to get philosophical. I want to get my bat and knock a rock for luck into the valley, into the long view the kid will have tasting this ontological fruit. I want to dig in and knock it all the way back to that river ancient tribes are still squabbling over—"

"Where you dropped your bag of apples and plums," Lizzie smiled.

"Yes, and where I knew, as a man knows only a precious few things in this mapped-over, flowing life, what your big surprise was."

"Did you really know?" she said. "Tell the truth."

"I had to," I said. "What could be bigger or sweeter?"

After we left Slovakia that summer and returned to Des Moines, we sold the house there and packed. We loaded a moving van with 14,000 pounds of stuff, including one of those iron-wheeled wooden flatbed carts you used to see in railroad stations—and still do in the Old Country—and almost two tons of books. Then we traded our Honda for a pickup and drove West, Oshkosh complaining on the floor between Lizzie's father's old red cowboy boots.

Three days and 1,541 miles later we rendezvoused with the van in Grangeville. The driver said he couldn't get his rig up our curlicue mountain road. So we hired a smaller van and two men and hauled the stuff up in relays. One of the men, Carlos, a short cheerful Basque who could lift anything ("Okay, okay, I hold it!"), puzzled over Lizzie's fragile antique hutches and cabinets. Why didn't we want new, strong? Because we have you, Carlos, Lizzie said—an answer which both satisfied him and renewed his vigor. Anyway, we got that part done. Then we planted our orchard. And split a beer. And settled on two names, Theodore or Margaret, depending. We didn't want to know until the actual moment.

For the actual moment, we had another long trip ahead. Or rather back. Since we never expected to have children, we hadn't arranged for any maternity insurance. Then Lizzie read the fine print on a policy she had taken out years before we met, and which we still kept up. We were covered, it turned out, but only in Iowa. So on 8 December, two months after we moved into our cedar house across the valley from Blacktail Ridge, we got in the pickup and started for Des Moines. Lizzie's parents would take us in to await 12 January, the predicted actual moment.

This time, rather than repeat the South Dakota–Montana route we'd taken out, we dipped down through Wyoming and Nebraska, figuring the weather would be less wild. Passing signs that said Diamondville and Opal, Rock Springs, Reliance, Bitter Creek, and Medicine Bow, I felt right at home: here, once more, I thought, were pieces of that moveable poem that we chase after and join and leave and get sentimental over and tell ourselves that we really know it. And sometimes, at moments, we really do, don't we?

Lizzie said, "I never want to live in another city."

Near Ogallala it began to snow hard, and by North Platte we were driving in a classic whiteout: for more than 100 miles we saw nothing on the road except six horizontal fuzzy red lights straight ahead. They turned out to be the taillights of a flatbed truck hauling coils of steel—a truck low and heavy enough to stay on the road, plowing a path for us. How could *he* see? That night we arrived, drained, at Greg and Barbara Kuzma's house outside Lincoln—a house filled with candlelight, beaming faces, warmth, dinner waiting, and Greg, in a Santa cap, handing us cups of hot cider.

The rest of the journey was easy, except for the main part. This baby—in utero—who had crossed the Atlantic three times, traveled more than 3,000 miles in a pickup on either side of the Great Divide, ridden up and down our mountain dozens of times as Lizzie and I, on foot, sought out fallen trees for firewood that autumn, seemed perfectly happy to stay put, nice and warm. It *was* cold in Iowa—every day a new record low. At one o'clock in the morning on 18 January Lizzie's water broke, and thirty hours later, after a lot of heavy Lamaze breathing on her part and encouragement from Gretchen and me, the doctor, going as far as he could to let Lizzie try for a natural delivery, finally called in a crew and performed a Caesarean. The *Des Moines Register* produced a rare two-banner headline front page that morning: SIBERIAN EXPRESS ROLLS IN and VICIOUS EARTHQUAKE SNARLS L.A. Never mind L.A. Margaret was born on the coldest day in Iowa in the last hundred years.

Two weeks later we bundled her up and drove back to Idaho—over the northern route.

In the earth-breath of my barn, in the woodshed where I split and stack years of flicker knocks and owl hoots, out in the piney air my corral keeps fresh, I cannot stop my arms from flapping—like a cock pheasant all feathered up, I'm about to fly yonder across the valley to Blacktail Ridge, give that old buck goat watching me something to see, a man with a new daughter, a father whose first-born came to assist at her sister's birth, stroking the mother-pain, embracing, bringing back how her hands fluttered to my cheeks when I bent close, how she fell from pure abandonment dancing in the grass to clutching my chest while the doctor sewed up her slashed foot, how twenty-eight years slipped by, her flight into photos and notes, calls in the night sometimes thousands of miles from where each of us felt the spinning, returned now as this random late snowflake comes down the mountain and catches my wrist, allowing me a moment to hold and praise no matter where I turn or how hard I wave, going sweetly mad at its intricate joinery, its own sweet praise and departure.

Early Spring: The Cougar

Up the mountain about eighty yards from my corral, in a thick growth of old and young pine, on ground spongy from years of brown needles, lay the deer's remains. All the good meat was gone. Two days before, near dusk, when I first saw the bright red color, I had not gone close to it—had not wanted to go in there under the low branches—for I suspected that this was a cougar kill and he might be returning to it. Now, observing the small pile of shiny intestines and undigested grass (none of which a cougar would care about), plus the scratch marks on a fallen fir right beside them, I had no doubt.

The first time I saw the cougar I was cooking oatmeal—that bright winter morning when Lizzie, upstairs nursing Margaret, called down for me to look out the back door—hurry! I went there and saw a snowshoe hare racing toward the house, upright, like some Disney dervish, its ears and all of its limbs in a whirl. After it disappeared from view, I heard Lizzie say, "Oh, look—above the corral!" There, stretched out in regal profile, was this magnificent tan cat, its long ropy tail lazily rising and falling.

My business above the corral the day I first saw the dead deer was to remove some hogwire. Joe and Jane, the previous owners, had kept small livestock up there. I had no interest in raising anything on that heavily wooded part of my land except what wanted to grow there on its own. I was also tearing down a blind that the eldest son had built. It felt good clearing out this stuff. When I finished with it, I said to myself, I'd do something about those young pines fighting for space. That's when I saw the bright red color, its sudden, heaped-up assemblage. I did not think, right away, of anything dead. I thought of "red," "curves."

I told Lizzie about the kill. I said we should keep Henry and Ella, our young dogs, in the run when we were not outside with them.

That night, in bed, Lizzie called my name. I said, "What is it?"

"You were yelling."

"Yelling?"

"Almost."

Then I remembered my dream. I had been invited to give a guest sermon to a congregation of religious geographers. I told them I could not believe in their instruments and ways of measuring everything down to the smallest clod of dirt. Their maps, for example, were too crowded, covered with too many pins and sighs. I meant to say *signs*. "It's very confining," I said to them, "nobody can move—nobody wants to move. Get outside," I advised, "walk around." Then I said, pontifically, "But I do believe in truth."

I reported all this to Lizzie.

"What did they say?" she asked.

"They didn't seem to understand my point."

"Were you polite?"

"We were all polite, that was the problem."

On the third day after finding the dead deer, I took a shovel up the mountain to bury what was left—three shank bones with their hoofs, a length of spine, a rug-like piece of fur. Lizzie accompanied me, shaking the bell on her walking stick and holding the pepper spray—just in case.

"Where do you think the other leg and head are?" she said.

"Dragged off," I figured.

I piled what was there onto the shovel and we hiked up the mountain another fifty yards, where I dug a hole. I didn't want to bury the remains where I'd found them. I still planned to work in that area, thin some trees, clear out dead brush and the last of that hogwire. I just didn't want a grave there. After covering the hole, I pulled some fallen tree limbs over it.

"I think we can let the dogs run free now," I said.

Next morning, I found Henry chewing on a bone in the yard—a two-inch piece of spinal column. Ella lay on all fours watching him. Henry and Ella were the produce of an Australian shepherd and a male rottweiler that jumped a fence it wasn't supposed to jump. They were still in that gangly stage. I took the bone away from Henry. I put the dogs in their run, then hiked up to my burial site. It was undisturbed.

That afternoon Charley Dreadfulwater brought me a cord of firewood. I told him about the kill. He said, "Anymore, you don't know what to think about lions. Used to be, you'd never see them, just their markings. Now their fear seems to be gone.

I was up in The Gospels. I got out of my truck and here were three of them standing on a ridge sixty feet away looking at me. Calm as anything. I eased back into the cab and had to wait maybe ten minutes before they decided to go away." He glanced over at the run beside the barn. "It's good you've got those dogs. Especially with a youngster to raise. Two dogs are a good thing. I like lions. I mean they were here first. But there's only so much land."

He looked around. "You butt right up to National forest. They've got clear sailing through here. Tell those dogs to hurry up and grow."

The next morning Henry had a shank in the yard. So he had found the fourth leg. I took it away and added it to the trash bag in my truck. To make sure this leg was not from the grave, I went up the mountain. I took Henry and Ella with me and carried, feeling alternately prepared and stupid, a pitchfork. The air was cool. I could see a white dusting of snow on The Gospels. I liked mountain lions too. I liked the idea that one would come and go on my land, using it to keep alive. I also wanted this animal to be properly afraid of me and my kind. There was a huge lion—eight or nine feet from nose to tail tip—stuffed and encased in a glass box at a gas station down near Kamiah. You could look at it while you pumped your tank full.

This time the grave was open, the rug-like piece of fur thrown aside. A crow sat above us in a tall Douglas fir and cawed, not happy. I brought the skin down and added it to the trash bag I would deposit in the county dumpster. I didn't want the dogs to develop a taste for deer. We gave them bones—beef bones from a butcher in town—that Lizzie boiled first.

My dream about delivering a guest sermon returned. I had been brought back to the geographers to explain myself. I said, "Look here. Look at this. It's very basic." I didn't like the sound of my voice, its all-knowing tone. I wanted to say, "I'm puzzled by things too. But so what? Isn't there a richness in—in—" I gave up. It was all very clear to *me*.

When I found the two pieces of jaw in the yard, I sat down with them on the bench beside the barn. The tiny front teeth reminded me of a bully I knew in grade school, though his teeth were even smaller, almost like rice. How odd to go from a deer's front teeth to a bully's. Maybe because—it occurred to me suddenly—when I finally turned on him and threatened to break his nose, he ran, startled. Something like a deer. And like a cougar ought to behave.

"If a lion really wanted to jump you," a ranger once told me, "you'd probably never feel it." Looking at the jaw bones, I figured that was fair enough.

The first time I saw that beautiful animal, there was a note of the burlesque, the ridiculous, attending it—that funny whirligig the snowshoe hare made running for its life. And I did laugh. But I was stopped short when I saw the cougar. The second time I saw him, in the spring, we were close enough, it seemed, for me to whisper in his ear.

The cougar who prowls my mountain came down close today and looked at me in my corral. We looked at each other. A fine mist lay among the wild oats growing there and there he stood, not moving. I was on my knees. Over his shoulder I could see Gospel Hump an hour away, still covered with snow. It was quiet and raining lightly and my hands, which had been cold from pulling up thistles, were now warm. For a moment I wanted nothing more than to lie in the snow on Gospel Hump and slowly move my arms, making a great angel. Then I wanted my father to be alive again and see this magnificence with me—we wouldn't have to say anything, I just wanted to hold his hand. Everything was very clear—the pointy buds on my plum trees nearby, his eyes, the dark whorls the knots made in the boards of my fence. I wanted to see him shake his head in wonder. Just once. The way he did after finishing a tough job, or when he had to admit he was happy. I don't know how long the cougar stayed, but I was glad to see him turn and go back—he went back as smoothly it seemed as a trout in water—and I returned to my thistles, whose almost silky white root slips out so easily when it rains.

In the Presence of the Clearwater

Walking this land I live on, I hear wind brushing through big conifers, a pine cone falling branch by branch—*pwak! pwak!*—a tree creaking over an inch, a tumbling rock knocking against other rocks, the sudden flutter of a chukar's wings, and the South Fork of the Clearwater rushing down cold from Elk City—all great and modest actions, adventures inevitable and fine. Don't stop, my heartbeat says, don't stop.

Far off, I hear Sparky whinny. I step on a fir twig, crack it, am given one clear individual note—punctuation in a jumpy sentence—and think of Thelonious Monk stripping melody down to its essentials. Or it's the finger-snapping sound I remember my leg making, breaking, as I slid into third base all those years ago. A crow's harsh caw goes up. Then nothing for a while. Then a wild turkey's outraged fussy complaint. Then only my heartbeat, *tha-thumpa, tha-thumpa,* that little rubber drum a kid is happy to beat, keeping time, on his determined way somewhere.

Sparky whinnies again. He belongs to Grover, my neighbor, who takes him elk hunting. Grover walks, Sparky carries the pack. They are a pair of toothy old sunburned grunts, Grover will say, pressing his grizzled cheek into Sparky's: "Look at us and tell the difference."

I make my way down from the high timber toward Grover's place, but halfway there I veer off. A large punky stump I know in a sunny clearing—around which blackberry bushes push up from the rocky soil in abundant sprawl for the bears to come and get fat on—is where I want to sit for a spell, and whittle, and watch the river.

I can watch it for a long time, even at a distance, and get lost and located simultaneously, and on this day I am soon carried over airy bright rips of spray to lathered horses I have known, how like fresh-crushed oats they always smelled, how the hard block of salt I chipped a sliver off—from the cup their tongues licked out—tasted hot. Then I am wearing a cast on my leg, using a straightened wire hanger to ease down the length of it to get at the itch. Then I hear, standing behind a furnace, the hiss of a water pipe, and feel Delphine Bononi's woolly rabbit-fur sweater pressing my heartbeat. I am in the seventh grade. No perfect tumble into sleep after fierce play, no race to raise my arm and shout from the highest, most willowy limb, no dive daring my hilarious lungs to hold out, hold out against the water's weight—not one of the world's roaring gifts that I knew compared to this, my first real kiss.

It changed the meaning of my mouth, the way I took small or great breaths forever, and if only for an instant it flares in the rippling mountain heat surrounding me, alive as anything given up wholly to a pure shimmer already slipping away, intact as nothing I can hold, a current leaving—and leaving behind, in the bright bone oven of my aging skull—one cool, finny, adolescent shiver.

Moments later I have to laugh, remembering the fiery sulfurous stink and sad, shriveled-up look of my leg after the cast came off. Then in the sunny clearing where I sit, a single honey bee declares itself to the slim Canadian thistles, to that purple blossom Sparky loves to eat, working his lips like the toothless old. I watch the bee swaying, taking its drink, while overhead a red-tailed hawk soars slowly, slowly under our brazen sun, over the South Fork's careless purpose.

For all this, I thank and praise the river, if those are the right words, and despite my urge to descend farther, to get closer to it, I can manage only to slip off the stump and ease myself into a prone posture of utter luxury, of near floating, using the soft composting fir for a pillow. I can hear the river, and that's rich enough right now. I am a citizen of that country where flow and swirl and sift produce, over and over, the perfect anthem and its response. Please do not salute yesterday or tomorrow too much, it says.

The truth is, I harbor sweet envy toward the river. Who can compose and sing like that? And carry on? And flout, caress, turning you to the moment? The subtleties in the song seem so easy. It copies no one, does not have the clicky tic for instant information, asks for no stars pinned to its bib, needs no diploma, no curriculum vitae, no fashionable shoe. Standing at our bedroom window, Lizzie and I can see a passage of it, a section of curled brilliance that on moony nights sounds like a woman removing and collecting in her palm, dreamily, a long string of favored pearls.

"Listen," one of us always says.

The first summer we lived on our mountain, Lizzie and I put in our first garden, on a knoll close to the house. I turned over the soil with a spade—an act, it was shocking to realize, I hadn't performed since I was a boy in Michigan. I shoveled up all the good aged-black horse manure from behind the barn and we spread it on the knoll. We also spread some steer manure from our neighbor Fred's pasture down the mountain. I bought a tiller and went over the ground again, making it look like dark brown sugar. Then, using old unpainted barn siding, we built three raised beds. We left space below the lowest bed for a sandbox. When we got thirsty, we drank from the spigot at our well—water that tastes like water, straightforward as spring. We planted carrots, spinach, beets, and peas, plus a dozen Early Girl tomato plants from Rickman's nursery in town.

"Fence up yet?" Alice Rickman asked.

We didn't have a fence up. We had two lengths of two-by-four nailed together in a cross, the long end stuck in the ground, the crosspiece fitted out with one of my sweat-ripe shirts and a pair of gloves, and an old Tigers baseball cap fixed where a head ought to be.

"That might keep the rascals off," Alice said. "For a time anyway."

So around the knoll Lizzie and I put up non-climb field fence, hung on ten-foot larch poles. To anchor the poles, I dug two-foot holes—eleven of them. Probably I should have dug at least three more, but those eleven took me almost half the summer. Right under the topsoil, dammit, ran a vein of granite exactly where I wanted to run my fence.

I worked on the holes every day after lunch—while the sun shone and the garden grew. My main tool became a homemade pile driver, a length of iron pipe filled with concrete. Straddling the target on my knees, I thrust the pipe down like a spear, chipping away at my mountain. Some days I was mad Ahab—or an Olympic athlete in a new, slow, sweaty event over which the TV sponsors, seeing their audience yawn, lost hair.

The holes dug, Lizzie helped me fill them with soupy cement that we mixed in the wheelbarrow, then helped stick in the larch poles. Two days later, everything firm, we began hanging the fence. Margaret, strapped in her stroller and wrapped to her eyes like a Slovak baby, watched us or snoozed. Oshkosh did likewise.

The six-foot fencing came in fifty-foot rolls. We measured our knoll to take exactly three of them. After nailing one end of the first roll on a pole, I scooched it to the next pole, where Lizzie hooked into the wire with two claw hammers about a foot apart and, using the pole as a fulcrum, pulled hard, holding the tension, while I nailed in fence staples between her hammers. Then she moved them up the pole another foot for me to staple there.

"A couple can get to know each other on a job like this," she said.

"Having fun?"

"You ever hang fence with a woman before?"

"Not that I recall."

"It's kind of sexy. All this holding tight and so forth."

"I'm glad your mother can't hear her former cheerleader-sorority girl-Junior League daughter talk like that."

"Anyway, if you have, keep it to yourself."

We took three afternoons—one per side—to hang the fence around the triangular-shaped garden. We could have done it in half the time, but the job and our pauses were too rich to rush. In one pause we gathered up Margaret, snacks, and our bathing suits and went down to the river, to wade in off a small beach, get closer to the subtleties—that humming, a rainbow nosing by, pebbles plump and bright as mushrooms on the bottom. The baby, reaching, wanted more. I took her hands. Held her up and slowly let her down, up and down, her tiny feet and mine together in a row. She squealed to see hers big, then small, then smaller. On the beach, Lizzie crawled in circles, clawing up a castle. "Maybe I am dreaming after all," she said.

In another pause, a corollary to the first, Lizzie would sit against a larch pole and nurse Margaret, positioning herself to keep her breast, though not Margaret's eyes, in the sun. I would dump a cup of drinking water over my head and lie back among the tomato plants, inhaling the mixed scent of milk, pine boughs, and those spicy green leaves brushing my ears. "I like this," she said. I listened to the sucks of outright pleasure, the easing off from one nipple, the arrival at the other. "I wonder if Gerard Manley Hopkins ever considered that a good example of sprung rhythm," I said once, and she said, "Like to try it?"

The West, contrary to cowboy lore, is not all reticence.

"Hey!"

I glanced up.

"Easy, buster."

The main purpose of the fence was to keep deer off our vegetables, but when spring came again and in the raised beds tiny spikes of green appeared, and the morning glories wound in the wire pulsed up and started to push out those pastel cups, and the sun sliding over Blacktail Ridge picked out the single drop of water clinging to the well spigot and created a large bristling effect not unlike heat lightning, I thought I might just open the gate and whistle the rascals in, to compare horns, to stamp my front hooves like they do, breathing the nutty odor of musk in the making that would drive us all—and surely it would—a little bit crazy about ourselves.

Those seeds produced. The carrots and beets were small but tall on flavor. The peas and spinach did even better. The Early Girls did the best. You can forget what real taste is after you've been eating those blatant frauds hauled over the highway in chilled darkness.

As for the sandbox, I took two ten-foot larch poles that I didn't dig holes for—the smoothest two—sawed them in half, and laid down a square. Then we brought up sand from our favorite neighborhood beaches. It is all fine stuff, full of the sun's brassy swirl and the earth's rhythmic sift, like a lot of things around here. Margaret, beginning her toddle, falls joyously in the middle, grips little fistfuls of it, and says with her huzzas: Yes, we may continue.

A very good word, *continue,* and from such a nice family. Continual, continuance, geese flying over again, right over our flapping arms, crossing the river and its glister and all these flickering grains. What could be more graciously willful? Lizzie and I have no trouble getting into this pleasure from time to time—there's plenty of room—and when we come out, as if from a rapids, we're ravenous.

Beginning My Education

Go back. A long time ago there were two bourbon-colored Belgians, great big steppers that could strut beside a row of beans precise as ballet dancers, trailing a flock of white birds. And engineering the show, my grandfather. But first he must leave the Old Country and come to Detroit and marry a Polish-American girl from Hamtramck—Angeline—whom he called Nelly. He said poems to her, poems by the heroic Adam Mickiewicz. And told her such tales! How could my grandmother ever forget Queen Wanda of Kraków who, pursued by a German prince, leaped from her castle window into the deep waters of the Vistula, calling out with her last breath that she would rather marry a Polish river!

When they went walking Sunday afternoons in Detroit, keeping away from the traffic of cyclists and especially away from those powerful new machines that came along more and more now and made such a noise and threw oil on the driver—and on anyone else who got too close—and worst of all, from Angeline's point of view, spurted red flames, Stefan would wrap her in an arm and raise his fist, saying that the great and beautiful way to travel was by *kon!* By horse!

She was sixteen. He was a blacksmith, trained to shoe the animal he loved, but instead he found work in Henry Ford's foundry, tending its fires. One day the accident—the splashing molten steel. The scars on his cheek, neck, and back, years later when I saw them, were like flowers, pink peonies, pressed to his skin.

In 1927, along with thousands of others, my grandfather looked at the sky and could not stop. He took his family north and into—my mother said—his dream. And the farm he bought, a rolling, mainly wooded place with a good stream moving through, was perfect for a dream—far better to look at and breathe in richly than to work. But when the stock market crashed two years later, he had to work it. Hard.

He was still working it when, at the close of the Second World War, I began spending my summers there. I was a city kid, from Flint, and much that I remember about that time seems tethered to Prince and Nelly—even the rosy lump I wondered about on the neck of the old farmer kneeling bent and nut-wrinkled in the front pew of my grandparents' little church. *An egg,* Grandma whispered (not wanting, I'm sure, to get into goiters during Mass), and I believed her, remembering the raw potato Grandpa carried in his pocket to help loosen his stiff leg as, draped in reins, he walked behind those full-rumped Belgians, crooning to them.

When he took them down to the creek for a drink, I too went down. But first—

I remember the woolly itch on the back of my neck from the scapular Grandma gave me, the Holy Family patch at one end, the Bleeding Heart at the other, one of them dangling past my belt and getting in the way when I had to pee fast, my shoulders and back prickly with hay and sweat. I remember running plenty ahead of Grandpa and Prince and Nelly and the hay cutter, my shins red and sore from kicking the cut stems, following beside the unmowed edge with my burlap bag flying—jumping over mice and garter snakes all snipped up in the cutter's wake, jumping over the sudden bright scatterings of new-born rabbits I didn't catch and run with to the bee-stippled orchard, among the windfallen Goldens, the spongy snows, and release; can remember and now almost touch the cold sweaty Mason jar of spring water waiting in the shade under a tree, can see myself wanting to lift it with both hands to my mouth, like him, the drops of water sparkling in his mustache, and wishing I too had a mustache I could wipe with the back of my wrist.

Now I see him pulling off the salt-slick harnesses and slapping the horses' withers and flanks, letting that big-knuckled hand linger on their foamy hindquarters; and now I can smell them, the sharp, sweet, barny odor of punky wood, old shoes, straw, and my own skin after running, waiting, and now I am cantering beside them down to the creek, into the creek, the wide hole where trout flash, the fine hairs on my face flat on the water, like Prince's, like Nelly's, like his, collecting bubbles, our muzzles in deep at last for a long, long drink.

Then my grandfather stood. Up to his hips in current, he pulled off his shirt and bathed those flowery shapes on his shoulders and back, shaking his head, a wild man slapping his sides, snorting—throwing one arm over Prince and one over Nelly who, up to their own hips, had been waiting for him to do just that. Although he was in his sixties, near the end of his life, to me my grandfather, exactly like those two companions, was of no age; he was a force, a collection of motion and silences and sudden bursts of sound that, were I smart enough then, I would have known was music.

Once more I join him on the hay wagon, and hear him click his tongue. To move Prince and Nelly along—along faster! Calling *Gee!* and *Haw!* until Grandma appeared, flowing, enraged . . . and he, his hands over mine, helped me steer the wagon around and around her, heightening her color further; and all the while a fine gold shower of hay dust falling, and he singing those sounds of recklessness and affection, that operatic dip and rise of murmur and huzza, to her, to me, to the magnificent team (look at them! his proud arm proclaimed), and all of which I can still hear when I am happy.

Then, the honeyed glow from the kerosene lamp on the kitchen table softening his scars, he began to disappear. He did this so quietly and smoothly I could not believe he would return in the morning. Night after night in that mellowing light he ate his soup and bread, he knelt on the floor hunched over his rosary like a small bear come from the woods, and from farther and farther away in his throat came the sound of recklessness and huzza ground down to a groan of satisfaction, as when he pressed his pink cheek into Nelly's or Prince's velvety lips, as when he tossed back the shot of whiskey he gave himself at the end of the day. Then from inside his shirt, where at first I thought he himself would crawl, he brought forth a book and was gone.

Grandma found him among the hollyhocks. Later he lay with pennies on his eyes, the shaggy mustache flecked with hay dust gone, trimmed to a small thing from nowhere I knew, his pink patches, his face, white and shiny as a bowl. Hot all over, I slipped away to the creek and took off my blue wool suit, and drank, and shook my head like a wild man, like a horse, and saw falling on the water nothing more than my skinny shadow.

Years later I learned of his love—it must have been love—for Joseph Conrad. Later still I would learn how much the two men had in common. But first I must climb the granary roof and straddle its ridge. Was there a better, richer perch from which to view eternity—pretending this was my mount and the oats under my legs pure gold—seeing all around me the worlds I might visit, the barn with its high haymow, the creek, the orchard, all good places in which to leap, bathe, swing from limbs—and seeing my grandfather come across the yard like a man learning to walk, searching his way? Suddenly among the pecking chickens he thrust out his arms, as if he were showing them how an acrobat performed on a wire. At the granary he stopped; looking up he seemed puzzled; then he smiled, waved, and went on to the barn. When he came out he was leading Nelly, bringing her over to me. I understood, thrillingly, that I was to get down from the roof and onto the back of something far better. It was the first time he had made this offer. I sat on Nelly's broad brown powerful back, holding her bristly mane, smelling that warm-woodsy-wet-oats skin, and yes, there *was* a better perch from which to view eternity—or at least the thing that it seems will go on forever—even though we only went slowly around and around and eventually stopped.

At no time during those three summers—nor at Thanksgiving or Christmas or any other family gathering—did my grandfather and I ever exchange a word. He patted my head, he gave me a hand up, he helped me steer, he waved. He worked a farm he had not intended to work so hard, and he read a complex writer who tried, above everything, to be clear, to make us see. He had two horses. When plowing his fields he trailed a flock of white birds that he seemed to have conjured out of the soil; when he milked, pulling those freckled teats, bubbled hearts of sweet clover rose in his pail. When he sat in the orchard looking at the sky, I would climb a limb and wonder what held him so still. I do not know what he thought—ever—except that in naming his horses he left a pretty good clue. When my grandmother told me he had once held her close and shouted that the great and beautiful way to travel was by horse, I saw him traveling by two, and shaking his head like a man who couldn't quite believe his luck.

Just a Boy

Grandma's parlor and kitchen were filled with candles and flowers and food, with old farmers smelling of whiskey and tobacco, their razor-nicked faces flushed red and their fingers thick as brown rope keeping track, bead by bead, of the sorrowful mysteries on their rosaries. All in Polish. I looked in the coffin—saw the pennies, the trimmed mustache, the clean white cheeks. I could hear him releasing those two angry breaths Grandma always swept me away from: *psia krew!* Sitting in a tree, or hugging the log bridge the cows crossed over, leaning way down facing the creek, watching my mouth reflected there and pretending to be mad, I never could make those pushy-breath sounds come out right. I asked my cousin Donny what they meant. He said I didn't need to know. But later when he was angry about something, he told me they meant *dog's blood*—only not to say them, they were bad. Why were they bad? They just were, he said.

Outside, my uncles Andy and Joe and Johnny passed a bottle, and smoked, and across the yard, his foot on the pasture fence, Donny looked at the black bull. I stood with Donny and looked at the chain hanging down from that wet nose. I remembered how it swung when he ran beside the fence, chasing me, and how it got caught in the barbed wire just in time. Grandpa came and unwrapped the chain from the fence and then held the chain in his fist and pulled and jerked more furious than I had ever seen him—as if he meant to rip it from the bull's nose. Their faces were almost touching. What he then said to the bull, all of his forehead the same dark red color, was nothing I couldn't understand—even if the words were Polish—because their sound was the sound of rage. It was what he did next that confused me profoundly. He pressed his red forehead against the bull's and held it there, the bull and my grandfather breathing through their noses like two fighters who have had enough but don't know how to simply quit and walk away from each other; and then he was whispering to the animal, or singing, or crooning, in a voice and tone not meant for anyone else, easing down to his knees in the dirt, as if he were next to his chair in the kitchen's honeyed glow, holding his rosary beads.

Years later—reading Conrad, reading about a man alone in the jungle—I sometimes saw my grandfather lifting his lamp and casting shadows in the low-dark, earth-smelling cellar, his breath also a shadow, while everyone else was gathered in the parlor opening presents.

Reading about a storm at sea, I sometimes saw him soaking wet, gazing out the barn door at lightning—his face streaked with it. And sometimes I'd see my mother, her face flushed as if she had just arrived in the orchard, newly married, for three days of dancing. "Oh!" she would clap her hands.

"What about Aunt Mary's wedding?" I said once.

My mother sighed and changed the subject to when they lived in Detroit and how much she loved riding the trolley—"up and down Woodward Avenue!"—which was the point of this diversion, the trolley ride, not the library and returning the books her father had read.

Years later, trying to straighten things out, weigh them, I knew that Aunt Mary had not been married in a church and then danced for three days in Grandpa's orchard as my mother did, but had simply met a man somewhere and produced Donny, and then lived a long time in a hospital that my parents and I took Grandma to in the car, bringing along the fresh tomatoes my aunt loved, which she ate sitting on a bench in the sun beside my mother and grandmother, while my father and I walked in the woods nearby. I understood that it was important for my father and me to leave them alone; that Donny was not happy pulling beans and forking manure because when he came in late from setting pins in town on Saturday nights and woke me up to give me a Baby Ruth, he would make a fist and shake it out the door toward the dark corner where Grandpa slept, and tell me that one of these days Grandma would sign the papers letting him join the Navy and not tell *him*. But I did not understand everything, Donny said, because I was a boy. And a boy, if anyone could tell him, would not understand that his grandfather—in the midst of all this—was a man who read books written to help us see.

One heartbreakingly beautiful fall day in the mid-1960s I was driving north from Flint to the Upper Peninsula and on impulse pulled off the interstate at Standish. I hadn't been to the farm in a long time. I could remember the big auction the autumn after Grandpa's funeral—all the cars in the yard, the old farmers, some with fingers missing, milling around in their overalls and billed caps, the auctioneer crooning over Nelly and Prince, stroking their haunches as if he knew them well, lifting their lips to show everyone their teeth—but I couldn't remember being there since. Surely I had been, I thought, falling into that kind of panic that sucks you down when you can't retrieve time orderly but only in random clumps. Surely when Uncle Joe brought Grandma to family gatherings in Flint and she made me promise to come visit her on the farm, surely I did visit, didn't I?

I was sweating a little as I drove slowly through Standish. I passed Fletcher's, where you could buy smoked whitefish and beer, hunting licenses and shotguns. I passed Wheeler's restaurant, where my mother always said Dad took her on their first date. Next to Wheeler's was Our Theatre showing *A Patch of Blue,* and around the corner the Arenac Lanes, where Donny had set pins on Saturday nights. I'd gone with him a few times and remembered how he'd hop down red-faced and grinning from his safe perch to gather the smacked pins, his naked shoulders bright with sweat—and how once, when we hitched a ride home in the back of a truck, he put those shoulders into the wind, toward the farm, and curled his biceps, as if showing the world how strong he was.

At the north end of Standish I passed St. Florian's Church and the cemetery where Grandpa was buried. I could have stopped in town to see Joe. I could have turned east toward Omer, seven miles away, and visited Donny and Aunt Mary. But I continued north, to the farm three miles straight ahead on M-76. My grandmother chose to live alone, though Joe looked in on her daily, and Donny, my mother told me, visited often. He had put his time in at sea, gotten married, worked for a while on the railroad, and now had come home. "To be close to Mary," my mother said.

I saw the black walnut and ash lining Grandma's driveway and almost kept going. I was not a good grandson. I was something else, a man who came to visit only on impulse—and not even to visit her so much as the farm itself. At the mailbox I turned in, my tires crunching walnuts and my windshield speckling with shadow and sunlight as I drove up the two worn ruts toward the yellow frame house. I remembered running down those ruts to fetch Grandma's mail—no, I'd run down on the grassy path between them because to step in a muddy rut might be bad luck! I wondered if my mother played such games when, courted by my motorcycle-riding father, *she* ran to that mailbox.

I didn't get out of the car right away. Something was going on, something so simple it took me several moments to see it. The old weather-beaten barn, where I'd played, had my adventures swinging from hayloft to hayloft like Tarzan, was leaning to one side—the whole thing on its way to rolling over, collapsing. Oh, it wouldn't fall today, or tomorrow, but when it did the swallows would flee from its rafters, great clouds of them, screaming as if for help.

I closed my eyes. I saw myself emerge from the barn holding one of Grandpa's bright red Prince Albert tobacco tins. I'd found it in a heap of harnesses and junk and had filled it with night crawlers from the manure pile to go catch perch and bass and pike. Never suckers—those we took the hayforks after, my cousin Ray and I, working squeeze plays on them at the wide, pebbly turn where the creek flowed shallow, flipping sucker after sucker up the bank and fiercely keeping score. Later, kneeling in the sun, we'd slice their bellies and, like crazy doctors, slip the long creamy tapeworms out. We tossed the worms at trees or hung them over posts to treat the crows, as up the hill we hauled our catch, going past the wet-nosed bull we bugged our eyes at, a-whooing at, but he just chewed his cud and drooled. At the pigpen we handed in our kill, quick to keep our fingers from the old sow's snout. Then to Grandma's garden for fat tomatoes, cucumbers, and radishes—and down the hill again to wash them in the creek, chasing schools of minnows with our cuke torpedoes. Suddenly we'd remember something and check between our toes for oily bloodsuckers. Always finding some we'd scrape them off with sand and pray that none had crawled in our ears or up our butts when swimming. On the sunny bridge we sprawled across the logs and ate, reciting batting averages. The truly great were always dead, except for the Splendid Splinter, Ted Williams, and smooth Joe DiMaggio. Then we'd sprint toward the woods, where our uncles every fall bagged their bucks. At the wood's edge, taking off our shirts, a leaf of wintergreen between our teeth, we'd lie on moss and lazily aim the sticks of birch we called our 30-30s—aim at everything and nothing—or just peel them, as if the stiff clean bark were paper and we had important things to say.

I got out of the car feeling light-headed, displaced, as you do after a powerful dream, and knocked on Grandma's door. No one was home. Back on M-76 I drove two miles to tiny Sterling—which seemed abandoned and ghostly—another twenty miles to West Branch, and by then I realized it was Sunday and Grandma was no doubt in church. I could have doubled back, waited for her, even spent the night. Instead I got on the interstate for the Upper Peninsula.

Ray was smiling, waving good-bye, in my head. Ray was Aunt Helen's boy, a year older than I, and like Donny not crazy about the farm. He would have preferred to stay in Detroit; he missed playing baseball, the new Ford his father bought, the pool at Rouge Park where you didn't have to worry about bloodsuckers! But for about a week he would make the best of a situation thrust upon him and dive in, and then his parents would come to rescue him.

So mostly those summers I was on my own, poking around, handling things, watching—following Grandpa and Donny as they did chores, doing a few easy chores myself like gathering eggs, feeding the chickens. Aunt Rita was still living at home (she was in high school then), and Uncle Joe was sometimes there, usually on Sunday afternoons, in the parlor courting the beaming Boots sisters, Jenny and Fran. He'd come home from the war "without a scratch," and always seemed to be smiling. Uncle Johnny was sometimes there, too, also home from the war, also a big smiler, but unlike Joe he carried German shrapnel in his knee and head. Sometimes he could feel it. "It swims around like a fish." But for long stretches I was by myself, and often in the barn. I liked the greeny smell of a cow's breath, the smell of sweaty harness leather and straw and raw milk, the aromas of feed grain, alfalfa—and I liked gripping the thick hayrope, like Tarzan, and swinging from loft to loft—

the crucial maneuver is beautiful Jane
about to be eaten from limb to limb
across that passage you call a river, only
your grip slips
on the rope you call a vine
and landing, dazed, it's not
a school of piranha you feel
but something inside.

The cracked ribs I suffered slipped from my mind within a couple of weeks and didn't come back until thirty years later when I was writing a poem—as other things slipped away and came back, long after the event . . .

I think of swinging down from the barn's full mow, the rope
burning my hands, the fork overhead with its three prongs

long as a man's arm tight against the pulley, descending
through dust- and feather-flecked sheets of fading light
and hearing my young uncle howling from the roof of the granary
hearing a late killdeer's last noisy shriek and hearing
my young uncle again under the close and giddy first star of
evening
howling he was stone-blind-gone-to-hell drunk on wheat wine
and what did the damn pigs and chickens and cows, what did
the damn bull think of that

I don't know, now, if that "young uncle" was Johnny drinking to escape a foxhole where for two nights, all shot up, he huddled beside a dead comrade, or if the howler on the granary roof was really my cousin Donny, who wanted Grandma to sign the papers giving him his freedom away from that place. I don't think it matters. Maybe it was both of them—and maybe they were only trying to sing as well as those birds.

A Song

It was a warm, soft, autumn-hazy afternoon, the season of harvest, and my mother was telling a Depression story I knew by heart, about working in the fields, of not having much, and then she added a detail I hadn't heard before. "I was so afraid of burning my skin, my face, that I kept rubbing Vaseline on it. I wanted"—she laughed at herself—"to be as beautiful, as fair, as those movie stars!"

We were sitting in her backyard, in Flint, splitting a beer, smelling the sweet scent of her apple trees. I said I remembered Grandpa at his forge, pumping the bellows to brighten the coals, holding in their red center the thing to be fixed until it too was red, then red-white, then pounding it into the new shape with a hammer, his face above the crimson pit the color of rhubarb.

She inhaled deeply. "That big Jonathan is loaded this year." And then like a poet accommodating whatever comes next, she said, "On Saturday nights, when we lived in Detroit, Pa liked his bucket of fresh beer. From that saloon up at the corner."

In many ways my mother is a poet. Weather, physical description, a good line are more interesting to her than strict chronology, getting names or dates right. "Sometimes," she said, "I didn't go to school because I had no shoes." When was that? "One winter—it was so cold the potatoes in the cellar were hard as rocks." How old were you? "I was a girl, a skinny thing—but my hair, no one had such pretty hair. It was the same color as Jean Harlow's." My mother's hair, for years the color of wheat, would be dull now if she did not dye it. My grandfather's hair was black, like his eyes. In the *American Heritage Dictionary* there is a picture of Joseph Conrad ("Original name, Teodor Josef Konrad Korzeniowski. 1857–1924. Polish-born English novelist and short-story writer") that shakes me. Cut the gray beard from his chin and replace the tie and tailored coat with a flannel shirt, and you have my grandfather looking off after he stood up, letting the bull go free, his nostrils flared and his black eyes shining.

"Remember that bull on the farm?" I said.

"I do. His eyes were just like Pa's."

My mother gazed a long way into the afternoon. "You know," she finally said, "those apples, even the years they get wormy, make wonderful pies, your dad always said. And they do. I'm going to bake us one."

Sifting flour, rolling out crust, she left the Depression fields and leapt to the wedding Grandpa gave her, the kind you don't see anymore. *Three* priests met her at the altar. "And Pa butchered a steer, a pig, chickens, he made that good sausage with garlic and pepper, and for three days people danced in the orchard. I'm telling you," she said, "we had fun." Then they were living in West Branch, where my dad was born, where I was born, where Gramps Gildner did very well building summer homes around Houghton and Higgins lakes for Detroit big shots, and where my mother and I had a very close call.

"One freezing day," she said, "I'm looking around at all the cold—the apartment, the building, the whole world's an iceberg—and guess what? I'm wrong. We're on fire." Well, I knew this particular story too—I had grown up with it. I lay in my crib, on the third floor, and my frantic young mother wrapped me quickly in her ratty muskrat coat and ran down through smoke and flames licking the walls, and didn't stop until she reached Frei Dieboldt's Garage two blocks away. Where she burst through a door wailing my father's name. I knew all this and in my mind raced ahead to finish the story for her—which of course had a happy ending. But once inside the garage, she suddenly added a fresh, huge detail. After all these years! There, at the exact moment, she said, was my father holding up the rear end of a Pontiac coupe that had slipped off the jack so Frei's other mechanic, who was underneath, could breathe. "This is true," she said, "don't look at me like a goof." Well, it might have been a less fancy kind of car, she admitted, what difference did it make? They lost everything, all their wedding gifts, clothes, thirty dollars she had saved in a jelly jar, what would they do! "But *you,*" she said, "you were howling your head off because your pants were full, which you hated, and were hungry, mad too, I was holding you so tight, and I was bawling like crazy myself, sobbing, *Ted! Ted!* And he just stood there blue in the face, that sweet man, couldn't talk, couldn't move, or that poor unlucky devil squirming on the greasy floor—you could only see his legs—would've got more than some ribs busted, and I didn't understand any of it. . . ." She took a deep breath. I waited for the happy ending, which had to do with hugging and thanking their lucky stars. But gazing off at the sun going down, sending out long red wings across the horizon, my mother only sighed, "Look at that, would you?"

What she did understand—not right then but soon enough—was that she didn't want to live anywhere in West Branch. Not in the apartment above Gramps' office in the lumberyard, which was where we moved next, and not in the little house we took after that. She wanted to live in Detroit, where people didn't keep tabs on every cough and sneeze you made, where Helen and Andy lived, where trolley cars and Hudson's department store and the Fox Theatre and Briggs Stadium helped make life *go,* and where my dad could do better than be a grease monkey.

"Let me tell you about Angie, the Italian boy your dad knew. Everybody knew Angie, nice looking boy, happy-go-lucky, he worked in a local café, fried potatoes, made the coffee, that sort of thing, nothing special. But what he could do that *was* special was play the piano. Weekends he'd play at a roadhouse by the lakes. Your dad would drive him and their girlfriends over—I didn't know your dad yet—and Angie would play and his girlfriend would sit beside him. And the last song of the night was always the one he wrote, which everyone wanted to hear, it was such a good song."

My mother, her eyes closed, began to hum, and then she sang, "'Sleepy time gal, you're turning night into day. . . .' Well, he wrote it for her, the girl sitting beside him, who was—well, who was as pretty and rich as a banker's daughter could be. And they were crazy about each other," my mother said, "just like in the movies. But her father, the old German, was against his daughter marrying someone like Angie, so he made her promise she wouldn't get serious about anybody till she finished college, and sent her off. Everybody said Angie should take his song down to Bay City and sell it and go to college too. It was a great song, he could make a lot of money from it, they said. But he wouldn't do that, he'd wait for her," my mother said, telling the story as if she had been there, been part of it, all along. "Besides, it was the girl's song! How could he sell it? So anyway, she'd come home for Thanksgiving and Christmas and the summers, and they'd go to the roadhouse, and Angie would play the song, and everything would be like always.

"Then one summer near the end she doesn't come home, doesn't come home, and finally she does. And you guessed it, she's already married, to somebody else, a college man, rich like she was. Your dad couldn't get over it. Here we were still in the Depression, times were tough, and the husband strolls into Frei's Garage in a spiffy white shirt—with French cuffs—and buys a new Pontiac. Pays cash."

"What happened to Angie?"

"He sold the song. Practically gave it away. I don't think he ever wrote another one," my mother said. "Everything was different."

A good decade after the Depression—after he and Gram moved into their new brick house on the wooded hill you could see West Branch from, and he drove his Hudson Hornet to the lumberyard where Uncle Carl and Uncle Ralph pretty much ran things okay, and he smoked his cigars and got Vi the bookkeeper to laugh—Gramps went into his bedroom one day and never came out.

Living in Flint now, we drove up north. I wandered around his woods. At the salt lick he'd put up for the deer, I worked a piece off with my jackknife, tasted the sharp heat. I found my dad under the hood of Gramps' Hudson; not knowing what to do either, he was checking the oil level, the water in the battery. I sat in Gramps' leather chair by the window (where once he watched the woods) and Gram came hurrying out of his room—walking like she always did, as if a pot were about to boil over on the stove—and then she stopped. Wiping her glasses so fast with her dress I thought her hand would fly off. Aunt Dorothy rushed over with a handkerchief but Gram wouldn't take it—didn't want Dorothy's arm around her either, she just wanted to clean her glasses. Then my mother and Aunt Jeanette came out of Gramps' room and Gram was crying now and they took her back in. My dad and Carl and Ralph followed. On the table beside his chair lay a pile of *True Detective* magazines, a pair of binoculars, a big pink seashell with a long woolly cigar ash in it.

Not then, but long afterward, my mother was telling me about a time when she and my dad and Gramps had just finished their lunch, and she was nursing me, and Gramps said he liked to see her do that, that Gram, a nervous woman, had always used a bottle. She also told me that for years Gram would not forgive her for being the one whose name Gramps had called, and the one whose hand he had held, at the end.

Shards and overlaps and brilliantly polished images—or furiously polished glasses—that take me here and there like a detective, like a dreamer, and mean what, exactly? When I pick up Gramps' binoculars, which Gram had put in my hands, I want to look through both ends—for the close, oddly hazy, almost smothering view, and for the far away and much smaller but sharper view.

I walk to the highest point on my ranch, from which I can see miles in the four known directions, and think of fire. The kind nobody wants around here. Let us burn our own, of our own making, that we can control. Then I think of the fire in a foundry that gives a man flowerlike scars, the fire of the sun a girl fears, the close and quite literal fire she later saves herself and her baby from, the fire in the heart of a boy who writes a song for a girl he will never win, the fire raging in the brain of an immigrant who watches the sky for hours, who wades hip-deep into a creek for a long drink, the dying fires of a lumberman who calls to a woman he had watched giving suck to a babe, and who, at his last moment, is perhaps wanting nourishment too, and warmth, and continuance.

Where Am I?

More shards. Although Stefan Szostak was born on soil the Poles have claimed for a thousand years, the birth certificate of his youngest child, my aunt Rita, says he was born in Austria on 27 November 1882. In 1882 there was no Poland, politically speaking, because Russia, Prussia, and Austria had conquered it and divided it into three parts, causing millions of Poles to emigrate.

Turning to Rita, I felt I wouldn't be floating off into romance as I do with my mother, and my aunt, when I called her and asked, told me what she knew. Pa quit school in the fourth grade, she said, and learned the blacksmith trade. He was a teenager when he arrived in America. His and Ma's birthdays were one day apart (she was born on 28 November 1886). They were married in St. Hedwig's Church—"quite young," Rita said, "twenty and sixteen." Which made the year 1902. In 1902 or 1903 they had a son named Karol, who lived three days. That was all Rita knew about him. He was followed by Stanley (1904), Helen (1906), and Andrew (1907). I was making an orderly roster, seeing faces. Aunt Helen offering me a chocolate rabbit. Uncle Andy lifting his glass, toasting "*Na zdrowie!*" But then a name I didn't know: Stella. Rita thought she came after Andy, but wasn't sure. All she knew—"but not from Ma, Ma couldn't talk about it"—was that Stella lived nine months. Then came Nettie (1910), Mary (1912), Jean (1916)—"it's possible Stella was born between Mary and Jean"—and finally Joe (1919) and John (1921). They were all born in Detroit. Rita was the only one born on the farm, in 1930, when Grandpa was forty-eight, Grandma forty-four.

"I'm looking at my remembrance cards," Rita said. Remembrance cards—from Catholic funerals—that give the dates of the departed's birth and death, the date and time and place of the service, the priest officiating, the site of interment.

I remembered driving to Detroit to bury Aunt Helen, three days after Christmas, gray snow, bitterly cold, my mother staring out the window, hugging herself. She said Nettie wouldn't be coming from Minnesota. "She's not feeling so hot." Nettie, my mother, and Rita were the only three left—out of eleven. "Well, I'm not feeling so hot either." She would miss Helen. Helen had been good to her, taken her in, helped her, showed her the ropes—even took a broom one time, oh yes, to this city slicker who was hounding her. Whacked the no-good over his head! And that trip to Hudson's—Helen's treat—to buy me a chocolate rabbit and my mother a hat, a gorgeous hat, and how I had slipped away from them, got lost, oh I was always running away—even when I'd grown up!—you can't change a leopard's spots. But Helen had taken charge and found me, cleaned off the chocolate I'd covered my face with, and then had my picture taken for Easter. "Oh yes," my mother said, "we had quite a time visiting Helen, always, always a wonderful time," and smiled, and began to feel better, she said.

Still more parts. After the First World War was over, Poland regained her independence and the heart of Frederick Chopin was brought home. He had been buried in Paris' Pere Lachaise cemetery in 1849—next to his mother—but now his heart lay in a crypt in Warsaw, in the Church of the Holy Cross. Like millions of others he had fled Partition, but now he was back, his great, romantic Polish heart was back—the heart that had produced the mazurkas and polonaises the Poles had held close when there was no Poland, when they could only hope. Now, with peace, they had their composer and their country back.

They had another hero back, the poet Mickiewicz, who had also fled and, like Chopin, kept Polishness alive from abroad with his art. He died in 1855, in Constantinople, rallying Polish legions against the Russians. The Poles had never forgotten Adam Mickiewicz, their immense debt to him, to his words. Statues of the poet—and of the composer—are everywhere in Poland. Mickiewicz lies in Kraków, in Wawel Castle, with Polish kings, his remains, like his countryman's heart, brought home after the great war.

Stefan Szostak at the end of that war was thirty-seven. He had been in America at least eighteen years and had fathered nine children, seven of whom were living. He was tending the fires in Henry Ford's foundry, which was blazing hotter and hotter because Henry was selling Model Ts like crazy. He was not yet sending my mother to the library—she was only three—but wait, slow down. . . .

On a visit to Flint I tell my mother I've been thinking about when Grandpa and Grandma got married.

"Yes—at St. Hedwig's."

"I wonder if there's a picture."

"Of course. That beautiful one of Grandma, in the bedroom."

"I mean of both—or of him."

"You know, you've asked me this before, and I've looked, but they must have all burned up. Everything we had burned up in that fire—except you. Maybe Rita has one."

"I already asked her. She doesn't."

"Maybe Nettie has something in Minnesota. She was always a good one to keep a lot of mementos. What are you doing, writing a book?"

"I'm trying to understand a few things."

"What's to understand? It was tough back then—and terrible after we moved to the farm. My god, beans were ninety cents for a hundred pounds, and you got nothing—zero—for eggs. All this talk is making me hungry. Oh, this is your fault. I wish I had some real kielbasa. Pa used to make such wonderful sausage on Merritt Street. Not much fat. Lean. But he was such a soft touch, he gave most of it away. How could we live that way?"

"He was a butcher in Detroit?"

"Of course! Before anything else. But no heart for business. Gave half the profits to relatives, friends, our neighbors on Plumer, anybody who couldn't pay. The Modarskis, the Kapanowskis. But they had twelve kids."

"Who did?"

"The Kapanowskis, I don't know how they did it. Let's see," my mother says, "they had Lillian, Clara, Mary, Martha, Josephine, Jeanette, Antoinette, Eva, and the three boys, Benny, Joe and Mike. How many we got?"

"Eleven."

"Somebody's missing. I don't know who. But somebody's always missing. There—go write about that."

The Kapanowskis owned the saloon where Grandpa liked to have his bucket of fresh beer on Saturday nights. My mother didn't tell me it was her Uncle Mike and Aunt Helen's saloon (Helen being Grandma's younger sister), but maybe she didn't care to dwell on this place where Grandpa met the realtor who sold him the farm that took her out of Detroit. I got this information when I called Nettie.

Twice widowed, Nettie lived in Longville, in the Chippewa National Forest, about 200 miles north of Minneapolis. She and Whitey Lynch, her first husband, had a wild rice business and a little fishing business. They also built a motel. I had slept in that motel, eaten their wild rice, and fished with their sons, Jerry and Tommy, in Little Boy Lake.

"That was such a long time ago," she reminded me.

I told her I wanted to go back even farther—to when Grandpa and Grandma got married in Detroit.

"Yes, at St. Hedwig's," she said. "Where all of us kids were baptized, confirmed, and went to school, too. The church and school were just up the street, on Junction. I remember the nuns in those heavy brown habits, only their little eyes and faces looking out."

Nettie said she left school in 1925, at fifteen, and that she and Whitey got married in 1928. "Pa wasn't happy, he wanted me to marry Polish, not Irish. You know, when Pa and Ma moved up north, I didn't go with them. I stayed on Merritt Street, with Grandma Mysliwiec, and worked in Mike and Anna Modarski's grocery store. That's how I met Whitey. He'd come in for lunch, because you could get a really good sandwich there, big slices of ham, beef, nothing like now. Anyway, when we decided to marry we drove to the farm. We stayed up all night with Pa, talking. A long night it was. That was 1928. And the next year, a week before the Crash, Jerry was born. I think I'm getting off the subject, Gary."

"So who were the kids that went up north?"

"Jean, Joe, and John. I remember it very well."

"Not Mary?"

"No, she stayed. Lived with my sister Helen, that good soul, then with Andy, you know, until they got tired of her. Mary was a little wild, but, anyway, who wasn't? No, no, Mary was okay."

I told Nettie I was having trouble finding a photo of Grandpa.

"Jean wrote me about that. I've got a million pictures, a lot of them cracking into pieces, but none of Grandpa. You should ask Rita. And Gary, please, come visit. Go fishing with Jerry."

I went fishing for my grandfather. How could he and the realtor meet in Kapanowski's saloon during that time? Prohibition killed the saloons. But maybe Kapanowski's establishment was really a blind pig with a heavy door, a peephole. Did Stefan and the realtor conduct their business behind a heavy door? And was Stefan still a butcher or had he gone to work for Ford by then, been burned, and was saying behind the heavy door to hell with Detroit? Saying with his pals that the war was over and all the Poles—the real Poles, including Chopin and Mickiewicz—were returning to the homeland? Surely there was excitement about the cease-fire, the future of Poland, the future. And when, in 1919, his son Joe was born—after a string of three girls, four counting Stella, the one his wife couldn't talk about—maybe Stefan saw in Joe's birth a sign, a sign for change. And though *he* couldn't go back to Poland, not with all those mouths to feed, maybe he could do the next best—or next romantic—thing, and caught up in the notion and euphoria of the homeland, *land,* he began to think of a place away from where he was then, a city gone crazy. Was that Stefan Szostak's thinking? In an America whose powerful armies had finished a war to end all wars? Whose genius Ford had invented a system—the assembly line—to put millions of cars on the road and paid such good wages? Whose advertising boys were urging everyone to spend, acquire, and improve their kitchens, their faces, their lives? Get a car! An electric refrigerator! A mink coat! Put on lipstick, girls, smoke.

Where am I? Where is my grandfather?

That's him over there, in the corner, brooding by himself, trying to figure out something.

In 1914 the exile Joseph Conrad paid a visit to Poland and was almost caught there by the war. He escaped back to England, and the next year he wrote "this journey of ours, which for me was essentially not progress, but a retracing of footsteps on the road of life . . . It seemed to me that if I remained longer there . . . I should become the helpless prey of the shadows I had called up. They were crowding upon me, enigmatic and insistent, in their clinging air of the grave that tasted of dust and of the bitter vanity of old hopes."

Tell that to a Pole. Quote that to him. Never mind Conrad's great themes of isolation and alienation, of fidelity and human solidarity, because the Pole won't be listening. In August of 1987, exactly thirty-eight years after my grandfather was buried, I asked a professor at the Jagiellonian University in Kraków, "What does Joseph Conrad mean to the Poles?"

"He is not a Polish writer," the professor said.

"But he was born here."

"He did not write about Polish matters."

"The spirit in turmoil? Survival? Salvation? These aren't Polish matters?"

"He left. He turned his back on Poland. He wrote in English. Mickiewicz, Sienkiewicz, Milosz—these are Polish writers. Not Korzeniowski."

If Conrad was not a Polish writer, I thought, then what was my grandfather not?

Well, he was certainly not—as the world gauges these things—an important man. He was a blacksmith-turned-farmer. A small farmer who read books, who sat in his orchard gazing at the sky or stood in a soaking rage watching the heavens ruin his crops; a farmer who liked horses, who took a grandson for a wild ride on his hay wagon and a book by Joseph Conrad, that outcast, into his grave. He never bought his wife an electric refrigerator or a mink coat, and though an old Model T sat on his farm he never drove it; it sat in a shed for the chickens to leave an egg on the seat once in a while, and for another grandson to furiously work the crank, swear, and end up kicking a tire. If that motor *had* been brought to life, we could not have gone for a ride anyway because the tires were all flat. All Donny wanted to do was start the goddamn thing.

Work Hard and Die

St. Hedwig's sent me some information: the church opened in 1903, the school two years later. Andrew Szostak attended the fifth and sixth grades (1920–22), Antoinina attended from the third through the eighth grades (1920–25). Genevieve, Joseph, and John all started at the normal time and were in the fifth, second, and first grades, respectively, until 28 November 1927, when "the family moved." Their Detroit address was 4759 Plumer. No school record for Mary Szostak.

As for baptism records, I received this:

Helen	b. 3-4-06	Bapt.	3-4-06
Andrew	b. 12-1-07	Bapt.	12-1-07

Antoinina	b. 3-3-10	Bapt.	3-3-10
Mary	b. 8-13-12	Bapt.	8-25-12
Stella	b. 8-15-14	Bapt.	8-31-14
Genevieve	b. 9-14-16	Bapt.	9-24-16
Joseph	b. 3-16-19	Bapt.	3-23-19
John	b. 2-15-21	Bapt.	2-16-21

No mention of Karol, that first child who was born in 1902 or 1903 and lived three days, and no mention of the second child, Stanley, who was born, according to Rita's Remembrance card, in 1904. No Confirmations mentioned. Did my grandparents get married in St. Hedwig's? No, said the church.

November 28, 1927, was Nelly's forty-first birthday; the day before her husband celebrated his forty-fifth. Perhaps Stefan saw good luck in these anniversaries attending a major move—especially that heady year when flight and good fortune were all the rage. Lucky Lindbergh, the stock market, and Babe Ruth all pointing up. Janet Gaynor winning an Oscar for "Seventh Heaven." And my mother, though I'm sure she saw nothing lucky in the number, was eleven.

If she stepped out the door at 4759 Plumer and walked up to Junction, passed the heavy door of Kapanowski's establishment, passed through the shadows of two factories—Ternstedt and Cadillac—passed St. Hedwig's Church and her school right behind it, then crossed Kopernick and Kulick and Lola Streets, she would come to Michigan Avenue. If she paid her penny or two and boarded the streetcar, she'd soon pass Naven Field where the Tigers played (whose Harry Heilmann that year won the American League batting title), and then arrive in the heart of the city: Grand Circus Park, the Fox Theatre, Hudson's department store. Stunningly sleek fur coats hang on big-eyed red-cheeked dolls in display windows. The smell of food is everywhere, my mother's stomach begins to rumble, and she is sorely tempted to blow her carfare on a bakery treat and *walk* the rest of her journey. But she boards the Woodward Avenue streetcar, north, toward the Main Public Library two miles away, in her hand a list of books her father wants, and under her arm, safe in a bag, the books he has finished.

One day in 1927 she doesn't get off at her stop. She keeps going, past the library, past Grand Boulevard where the majestic Fisher Building rises up taller than anything she knows, and in whose cathedral-like lobbies she has bravely ventured and seen, in the polished marble lining the walls, her image, returned so richly, so elegantly, that she too has seemed beautiful and rich and elegant, seemed part of a fabulous story—a story she has been thinking up, continuing, each time she leaves Plumer Street and boards the streetcar and breathes in—everything! But she is not on the streetcar now, not in her story; she's in another vehicle and leaving everything behind. Passing through Flint, Saginaw, Bay City. Through Kawkawlin, Pinconning, Standish. Towns with dirt streets, no trolley cars. Then they arrive at this place he has brought them to: a lonely house, a smelly barn, gray sheds and gray chickens running around in the mud.

"When we moved," my mother said, "Andy took us in his Rickenbacker. He and Ma sat up front, us kids in the back. Pa rode in the truck he hired, with the driver. It was cold. It was always cold up north."

In a marsh area on the River Rouge (which flows into the Detroit), Henry Ford circa the First World War built a huge plant, commonly called The Rouge. An engineering magazine at the time hailed it as "all things to all men." At a distance I am following one of these men walking toward a river with a soft, feminine name, toward a modern wonder that contains blast furnaces, coke ovens, a foundry, machine shops, a body plant, sawmill, glass factory, cement plant, locomotive repair shop, paper mill; that possesses a fleet of ships—the *Henry Ford II,* the *Benson Ford,* the *Oneida* and *Onondaga*—which via the Great Lakes haul in iron ore, coal, and lumber from such Upper Peninsula reaches as L'Anse and Pequaming, and haul out Ford products via the Atlantic. I am following a man I think is Stefan Szostak to The Rouge because it is not far from Plumer and Junction, because it pays excellent wages, and because in its hottest rooms—which issue flames and a gritty red dust to the immediate sky—a blacksmith looking like almost anyone can be burned. And for a moment I see his face and shoulders, that mottled skin the raw color of a cow's tongue as he turns in the creek, removing his shirt and going round and round like a man in joy or in pain, bending over, way down, then slowly raising his head as if to call out, is calling out, though I can't hear him, can only hear from the far field a killdeer's fading *kill-dee, kill-dee,* and then from the top of that field, standing against a red evening sky, a black bull, moaning, announcing the stillness.

I am waiting to hear back from Darlene Flaherty. I had found her by making several calls to Detroit; she told me she was "in charge of seven thousand cubic feet of records that include just about anybody who ever worked for Ford."

"I don't suppose you'd have my grandfather?"

"Let me look."

Darlene Flaherty called back and said she had no Stefan or Steve Szostak of 4759 Plumer. But she had a Stanley and an Andrew of that address. She had the periods of their employment and the birth dates they'd given. (Both of my uncles added three years to their ages, to make themselves twenty-one at the time of employment.)

"But no Stefan, Steve, or S. Szostak," I said to Darlene Flaherty.

“I have another Stanley,” she said. “Born 1888. Worked in The Rouge furnace room.”

“How long was he there?”

“Eleven years—1916 to 1927.”

“What’s his address?”

“Twenty Saginaw Street. Maybe,” Darlene Flaherty said, “the personnel person misheard him. Heard, you know, Stanley for Stefan.”

My grandfather was born in 1882. In 1916 he was thirty-four, certainly not old, even then, but subtracting six years from his age wouldn’t have hurt, not if The Rouge wanted strong young backs in its furnace room. Also in 1916 Stefan and Angeline had six children to feed, including a new baby, my mother, and if he was an unsuccessful butcher . . . ? But what did Twenty Saginaw Street mean? Was it closer to The Rouge, perhaps in its very shadows, so that he could be on the job quickly, work extra shifts? Maybe he was even in on the construction of Ford’s wonder, a man with a strong back who rose from his bed and in a jiffy was on the job, helping to raise this place that was all things to him and to all others. I searched my street map of Detroit expecting to find Saginaw close to The Rouge, but found no street with that name anywhere on the map. Of course it could have been there in those days, and subsequently been swallowed up.

I called Aunt Sophie, Andy’s widow, who had lived in Detroit all her life. I asked if the Szostaks ever lived on Saginaw Street in the city.

“Saginaw? I think they always lived on Plumer. But Andy and I weren’t married until 1939, so I really can’t say. Yes, June of ’thirty-nine, and our Barbara was born in August of ’forty—one year before your sister Gloria. You know, Stanley’s Gabe might be able to tell you about Saginaw Street.”

I called my mother. "Now what?" she said. I told her I wanted to talk with Gabe. Did she have his number? "What am I, your information service? I've got a dead tree to cut down, walls to paint, a funny ticking in my old jalopy that might be a bomb. Gabe and Doris live in Texas. But you'll be lucky to find them there. They're always on the go, you know that. Europe, South America, name it. They're like the wind. They have a wonderful time, those two. They don't shut themselves up writing books! But if you do talk with Gabe, ask who's got that picture of his dad now, from the first war. Oh, how handsome Stanley was then, in that uniform, really it's a fabulous picture."

"Uncle Stanley was in the first war?"

"Oh yes."

"He couldn't have been more than fifteen."

"Well, I *saw* the picture."

Dialing the number she gave me, I remembered the last time I saw Gabe—at my mother's house at least twenty years before. He was smoking a cigar—"Cuban," he said—and sipping a brandy, clearly enjoying the illegal stogie and the little mystery of how he came by it.

He answered the phone. "You're lucky you caught us." He and Doris had just walked in the door after three months in Spain, and in the morning they were leaving again—to spend Thanksgiving in Florida. I told Gabe I was gathering information about the Szostaks, especially about those early Detroit years when his dad was a boy.

After a long pause, Gabe said, "My dad was more or less estranged from the family. They said he drank too much. And then too he married my mother. Nelly was against it, though Steve wasn't. You have to realize, in those days the children, when they worked, brought their pay home and gave it, all of it, to the parents. My dad was making good money then. So when he announced he was getting married and would pay Nelly rent, she threw his money at him. He left. Went over to Merritt Street and lived with Grandma Mysliwiec. He was nineteen, my mother sixteen. This was 1923. I was born in 1924 and lived the first eleven years of my life at Grandma Mysliwiec's, up on the third floor.

"Incidentally, at some point my dad changed the spelling of his name. To S-h-o-s-t-a-k. I didn't discover the change until I applied for my first passport."

I said, "My mother remembers a picture of your dad in uniform."

"When he was sixteen he joined the Army," Gabe said. "He served six months, I believe, then Grandma M. went and told how old he was and got him out. After that he attended Henry Ford Trade School. Which got him good jobs—at Studebaker, Pierce Arrow."

"Not at The Rouge?"

"He never mentioned it. You remember that Indian hood ornament on the Pierce Arrow? That was my dad's."

"He designed it?"

"He made the die for it. Then he got into politics and almost was murdered, but that's another story."

"Murdered?"

"A case of mistaken identity. I understand you've been to Poland. I was there in 'sixty-eight. Pretty gray. You know," my cousin said, "Steve was rather well off in Detroit. He owned at least two houses, maybe more. Oh yes, he was doing well before the Depression."

"Why would a man doing well in Detroit move to a modest farm up north?"

"You'd have to go inside his head for that."

"He and Nelly had two children that died young. Karol and Stella. What do you know about them?"

"I think Stella died in that big flu epidemic—1918? I never heard of any Karol."

"He was their firstborn."

"No, no, that one was named Stanley. When he died and my dad came along, my dad got that name."

For a few moments I didn't know what to say. Finally I asked if Saginaw Street meant anything to him and he said it didn't ring any bells. Then he was saying, "It wasn't easy being a Szostak. Every one of them was, well, almost a different type. And you know about Steve's temper. He was nothing like his brothers, Pete and Jake. They all came over from the old country together. Jake was a Jesuit—"

"A Jesuit?"

"Wore black all the time. Thoughtful man."

"We had a Jesuit in the family?"

"Always thinking, Jake was. But poor Pete, he had terrible luck, especially with women—three wives died on him."

Or they had terrible luck with him, I thought.

"Anyway," Gabe said, "my dad, mother and I were closer to Nelly's sister Anna and her husband Casimir. Casimir played the violin and French horn and did very well as a contractor. Until he fell off a scaffold and broke his neck. That was it. Everybody said he should have stayed with music."

I asked what he could tell me about Aunt Mary as a girl.

"She was with the group that moved to the farm," Gabe said. "She had trouble with her teeth. I guess from early on. She seemed to blame Steve and Nelly for not getting her proper care. In the 'thirties Mary would come to Detroit periodically and look for work. I think Jean would come with her. Andy also moved back and forth between the farm and Detroit. I'd only get glimpses of this, you understand, mainly from those summers I spent up north when I was a kid."

And Donny's father?

“I understood he was an M.D. that Mary became involved with when she was a patient in Traverse City. There wasn’t a lot of talk about it.”

“My mother wonders where that photo of your dad in uniform might be.”

“In a box probably.”

“Were you old enough to remember when Steve got burned?”

“On his face? Yes, that happened when he worked for the railroad.”

“Not in Ford’s foundry?”

“No, no. He got sprayed by hot steam—from a locomotive.”

I phoned my cousin Leonard Dobis in Florida. Leonard was the first of Aunt Helen and Uncle John’s three sons. I asked what he remembered about Steve. I was calling my grandfather Steve now as if I’d gotten to know him better, though in truth he seemed to be slipping away, or sideways, seemed like a character in a foreign film who makes a big first impression taking his time harnessing up a team of Belgians, confidently slapping their flanks as if he’s going somewhere important, only to reappear briefly in the bloody apron of a butcher, in a saloon drinking alone, in a crowd of workers entering a factory, on a railroad platform mostly hidden by the engine’s sudden release of steam. Or possibly standing on the porch of the latest house he’s acquired, thumbs hooked in his vest and grinning to let us know how well off he is. No.

Leonard said, “My folks were married in 1922. My mother was sixteen, my father thirty-three. Steve liked my father, who came over from Lithuania. I don’t know if he was Russian, Polish, or Lithuanian—my mother called him one or the other depending, you know, on her mood. Anyway, he had some money, about $3,000, not bad for that time, and Steve figured he could take care of her. He'd built a little house on Smart Avenue. No, not Smart, one block north of Smart. I'll tell you, I just brought the boat in from fishing, had a few beers. I'm retired now. In fact I got my first social security check today. I'm celebrating," he laughed.

"So they met at a dance, were married, and lived *near* Smart. Then in 1928, the year I was born, they moved to 5906 Renville. Jean lived with us too for a while, in the 'thirties. I remember Ted would drive down from West Branch to see her. I liked Ted. He'd take me for rides in his car. Up and down the streets, up and down, just looking at everything. Ted was the most easy-going guy. Nothing like the Szostaks. Not like Steve, that's for sure.

"Every summer from when I was nine to thirteen, my folks left me on the farm. The first couple of summers I had fun, then Steve put me to work. I was in the fields from sunup to sundown. At night my balls hung down to my shoes. To heck with this, I said. If I'm going to work I want to be paid. So I stayed in Detroit and got a job at the Statler Hotel. Then I ran away to Hollywood—that was 1944—to be a movie star. Oh man, nobody discovered me. So I went home, finished high school, and married Marge the same month I graduated—June of 'forty-seven.

"But I'll tell you another thing about Steve. He could stay up all night drinking and telling stories about the kings and queens of Poland. Story after story. I wish I could remember some. It was like he knew them personally, had lived in the castle with them. The kings and queens of Poland. Marge didn't even know Polish and *she* was impressed. Because he'd really get into these stories. After a while *he* seemed to be the story, if you know what I mean. His expression, the way he sounded, and also, don't forget, he was a handsome man. He seemed to belong in those romantic times. But he had that temper too. I saw him take a horse whip—a horse whip—to Joe and John one day. Complicated man."

I said, "I was just talking with Gabe, who said—"

"You just talked with Gabe? Where is he now?"

"Texas."

"That guy. I haven't seen him in years. Has anybody? And has anybody figured out what he *does?*"

"He's heading to Florida tomorrow."

"Nobody told me."

"He says we have a Jesuit in the family."

"No kidding, who?"

"Steve's brother Jake."

"Gabe should know."

"He also says Steve was well off in Detroit."

"Sure he was. Owned a couple of houses, maybe more."

"Why would he buy a small farm up north?"

"He was like my dad. My dad wanted to go back to Lithuania and buy a farm. They had this thing for horses and land, those guys from the old country. They all wanted to be gentlemen farmers. My dad just talked—and died in a rest home at ninety-four. But Steve did it. Only the Depression came along and he had to become a real farmer."

"What do you know about his accident at Ford's?"

"What accident?"

"He had those scars," I said.

"Scars? I never noticed any scars."

"On his face—that big pinkish patch—and on his back. He got burned," I said.

"If he did it must have happened when he worked in Wyandotte."

"I thought he worked in Ford's foundry."

"No, no, Wyandotte."

"What did he do there?"

"You got me."

"Who was Donny's father?"

"Oh boy, you're really. . . . Well, Mary was tied up with this Dapper Dan named—let's see—Charles. From Louisiana. Charles followed the horses. Mary would go to New Orleans with him. But I guess it happened when she was living on Alexandrine in Detroit."

"What did?"

"The romance. The beginning. Listen, this is old stuff. Come down to Florida, I'll take you fishing, tell you a good story. I've got all this material I've wanted to put in a book for years. I just need somebody to, you know, fix up the sentences."

I called Nettie back. I mentioned The Rouge, Saginaw Street.

"No, no, Pa worked at Ternstedt's. I remember walking with him over to Junction in the morning, holding his hand. Then staying on the corner as he went up the street. At night I'd run back to the corner and wait for him. How tired he looked, how—oh what's that word people use today to mean very tired? You know what I mean. It's—it's—oh I can't think of it. He had his dinner pail and his head would hang so low. I washed his feet for him."

I told her what St. Hedwig's said. There was a long "Oh." Then she sighed, "Life is funny, isn't it?" Then, "Maybe they were married in Wyandotte. Pa lived there for a while. When he first came over. Anyway . . ." she trailed off.

"Gabe tells me Uncle Jake was a Jesuit."

"Oh, Jake was a very good man. Very good. Always with priests."

"Do you know who Donny's father was?"

"I don't think anybody does."

I called my mother again. I said I was lucky and had found Gabe home and just wanted to tell her about Stanley's photo.

"So tell me."

"It's packed away, Gabe said."

"Stanley died too young."

"He told me about your uncle Casimir falling off a scaffold."

"Casimir, oh boy, he and Mike Kapanowski made a pair. One day he's on a ladder outside his saloon fixing something. Out of the saloon comes this good time Charlie, who yells, 'Hey, Mike! Hey, Mike!' and starts shaking the ladder. Down comes Mike and breaks his neck. Just like Casimir. The end. And poor Helen Kapanowski was pregnant too."

"Did you go to Nettie's wedding?" I said.

"Nettie's? No. Nobody did. Pa was mad at her for marrying an Irishman. She got married with strangers, the Modarskis, who ran that grocery store."

"Gabe says we have a Jesuit in the family."

"Who?"

"Uncle Jake."

"Maybe. He was always around priests."

"That picture of Grandma," I said, "in the bedroom, would you let me make a copy of it?"

"Why?"

"It's a beautiful picture."

"Why are you doing this, Gary?"

"Doing what?"

"Asking all these questions, collecting this stuff. We're nobody—nobodies—never done anything except work hard and die. Why don't you leave us be!"

A Snapshot

Aunt Sophie sent me a snapshot. I studied it, feeling both fascinated and troubled, and put it away. To take my mind off my family, to leave them be, I'd write a short story. I already had the title, "The Rug-Beater of Zoliborz." Zoliborz was the section of Warsaw where I had lived during 1987–88. On Saturday mornings I often stood at my window watching a white-haired man across the street clean his rugs, beating dust from the flowers and birds and sailing vessels woven into them. He was coming back to me, and all over again he seemed not to be knocking dust into the air so much as releasing color and scent and song, revealing to that oppressed and cheerless country a way of escape. If I could describe this well enough, it would lead me to the next thing, and the next, and I could leave my family alone. The only problem was, the old man of Zoliborz was turning out in my story to look like the old man in the snapshot.

I took it back out. There, in bright sunlight, are Joe, Andy, Rita, and Steve in the back row, Nelly and Donny in the middle, little Barbara up front. Everyone looks familiar—and true—except him. Why is his hair *silver?* My grandfather had black hair, like his mustache, his eyes, what's going on?

Aunt Sophie is taking a picture on the farm after church. The war is over. All the men wear white shirts and ties—Donny too—though only Joe is wearing a coat, a natty double-breasted pinstripe with a hankie in the pocket. Maybe that afternoon he has a date with the Boots sisters, Jenny and Fran. Tall and blond, Joe has the shoulders and good looks of an actor, a star athlete; he once, in fact, had a tryout with the St. Louis Browns baseball team. Lay a horse whip on Joe? Look at that jaw, this is a son who would do anything for a parent. Andy seems to be indicating just that, one hand on Joe's shoulder, the other on his mother's, connecting them. I can't read Nelly's face, it's washed in shadow, but she must be pleased; after all, it's Sunday and attending Mass always makes her feel good. Rita seems the happiest, the most relaxed. This is my Aunt Rita, always cheerful. What's her secret? Donny, also smiling, leans his head to the side as if Sophie says he's blocking Rita. His arms are too long for his shirt—he is at that age when people say to him, "You're growing like a weed!" But his necktie is very smart—striped silk. I remember it. "Andy wore it with his monkey suit when he married Sophie!" My cousin broke into a leg-slapping laugh. What was the joke? Andy dressing up like a monkey to marry Sophie? Or was the joke somehow on the boy who inherited the tie? I was hopelessly in the dark. "It always bothered Donny," Sophie said when I called to thank her for the snapshot, "that Mary wouldn't tell him who his father was. But he had all this other family, didn't he? Life must go on." That's right. And here's a bright spring or summer morning up north, Sophie and Andy's Barbara is standing with her handsome Uncle Joe, and the others, and a record is made of life going on.

Steve is sixty-two, in a vest, and though much of his face is in shadow I can make out a darker patch on his cheekbone. He is not smiling. He looks a little annoyed, puzzled. The one hand you see is big, a worker's hand. The ripples in his vest suggest a muscled stomach. He is not a foolish man, certainly, and I don't believe he would tell me that the shiny lump on the neck of the old farmer kneeling in front of us in St. Florian's was an egg.

No, not foolish, or misleading, and yet I could never tell my West Branch cousins that my Grandpa Szostak walked into his creek with his boots on and drank water like a horse, because they would probably laugh, as they did saying "Shoe Stack." Farmers didn't *do* things like that. Didn't sit around gazing at the sky or read books. The shadowy face of the strange man in Sophie's snapshot is the face of a reader; it's also the face of a man who could bend his back in a foundry, work double shifts, drink alone, brood, and, yes, use a horse whip. But on Joe? Or hook his thumbs in that vest to show what a clever businessman he was? Reduce his age from thirty-four to twenty-eight in order to appear stronger? Lead two lives?

Shards and overlaps. Images. You get something going with an old Pole beating dust from flowers, birds, and ships, releasing color and song and a way of escape, and pretty soon it's decades later, you're looking at a snapshot and wondering if the silver-haired man in the back row might take the name of a baby that lived three days, because life must go on.

St. Hedwig's suggested I contact St. Francis D'Assisi, north ten blocks or so from Plumer and Junction. Started in 1889, maybe St. Francis married my grandparents and baptized Karol/Stanley and Stanley. I called St. Francis. No—no Szostaks. "But," a secretary said, "maybe Holy Redeemer had something. It goes back to 1880." She added that she would send me a directory of the Catholic churches in Detroit that included their founding dates.

I called Holy Redeemer (located about eight blocks south of Plumer and Junction) and was given a woman named Lupe. I told Lupe what I was after; she said to call back tomorrow.

Meantime, I began to recollect a cold October day in 1948 when my grandfather stood at the foot of St. Florian's altar and in front of three priests draped in red and white chasubles—the colors of Poland—gave away his daughter Rita to Tommy Garbulinski. It was the same day I was slapped on the cheek by an old bishop, who wanted to remind me to be strong in my faith.

My parents and I that day made two round-trips between Flint and Standish, logging about eight hours in my dad's 1936 Chevrolet. We drove up for the wedding, drove back for my Confirmation, returned to Standish for the reception, and in the wee hours of the morning came home. My dad didn't mind this a bit. He loved to drive that '36 Chevy more than he loved anything, my mother said, you name it. A regular Barney Oldfield, she said. She herself was not thrilled to be cooped up in a car all that time, but what could she do, the bishop came first, dancing second. For God's sake, Ted, don't tell Ma you heard me say *anything*. Winking at me, he said maybe we wouldn't. But dance she did, after I was made a Soldier of Christ, because everyone was there, the whole gang!

We entered a Standish hall and it seemed to me as I was pulled into the full bosoms of my aunts, had my hand shaken, and the top of my head patted, that everyone on the Polish side of my family *was* there, plus many strangers, local farmers, and the priests in their collars. The horns and accordions up on a stage had most of them going, round and round, red-cheeked and whooping, dancing the polka, stamping the floor on the beat needing stamping, women with men, women with women, children with tipsy pot-bellied uncles, and bridesmaids all in a fluff kicking their shoes off—and off to the side, tables of food, kegs of beer, and waiting on the bar, lined up like tiny soldiers, big shots of whiskey. *Na zdrowie! Na zdrowie!*

"This is your Aunt Mary, Gary," and she took my hands and held on as if she were more glad to see me than anyone in the world, her face, like Rita's, ablaze—and these two sisters waiting beside the circle of dancers for me to say something. Hello, yes, I remember Aunt Mary, I went with my mother and dad and Grandma to see her in Traverse City, we took tomatoes, she loves them, her cheeks are that red, she ate one sitting on a bench in the sun, crying, and my dad and I went for a walk in the woods to leave them all be. But I only said hello, and sure, I remembered her. Still she held onto me.

I saw Donny walk by with a bottle of beer, loosening his tie. I heard Uncle John Dobis, Leonard and Ray's father, tell a story to which the men gathered around him said *dobrze, dobrze,* good, good, and which I would hear again, at other weddings, every time I saw Uncle John Dobis—hear that when he first arrived in this country as a young man, knowing nothing, still wet behind the ears, he had had the great luck to meet a wise priest, who said to him, "John, America is very rich but difficult. To live a long and happy life here, you must begin each day like so—relaxed—with a shot and a beer." How, my Uncle John would grin, could he ignore the advice of a priest?

Aunt Mary held my hands until my sister came by. Now she held Gloria's hands, my sister in her frilly white dress, Rita's flower girl, the two of them, Rita and Gloria, like *roses,* Grandma said, and Aunt Mary, her cheeks red as the tomatoes she loved, still fixed to my sister's small hands while Rita goes away, is taken away by Andy to dance. Beaming. Look at her, says Sophie, beaming herself, graduated from Sterling High a salutatorian, a star on the basketball team, she had offers—Sophie's voice rising—from a dozen colleges! Is Sophie angry? Or only trying to be heard above the horns and accordions, the dancers' whoops and shrieks? Tommy Garbulinski, Sophie says, is a fortunate man.

A Navy man, a chief petty officer, Donny says. He fought in the Pacific! Donny, someone laughs, are you dreaming again? But it's true, says another, it's all true about Tommy. And now he has such a good job down in Flint, at Buick. A foreman. A foreman, are you kidding? He's a supervisor!

I am punched on the arm by Ray—to follow him outside and play catch. It's so cold our gloves are stiff as cardboard. Uncle Johnny joins us. He fires one over our heads and the ball hits his Packard, spiderwebbing a window. Johnny laughs, says sniper fire. Ray wants to hear about the foxhole Johnny lived in for two days, pinned down by snipers, the dead buddy beside him; wants to hear about the Luger Johnny brought home from the war and which I have seen, unwrapped from an oiled rag—but you don't point it at anyone, ever, even if the firing pin *has* been removed, remember that. I do. As I will remember my mother saying—every time we saw the actor Robert Mitchum on a movie screen—"*That's* who Johnny looks like, only handsomer."

Donny appears at the edge of our game, not saying anything, just swigging his beer, listening to Johnny tell about keeping his head down for two days and trying not to piss on his dead buddy from Brooklyn when he couldn't hold it anymore. How close, everyone said, Donny and Johnny had become after

Donny served his Navy hitches and came home to Michigan and Johnny built a cabin on the farm. Aunt Elsie in Wyandotte was practically a widow, they said, he spent so much time up north fishing and hunting. Well, why shouldn't he quit the factory and enjoy those woods, my mother said, his leg so stiff now from all his wounds, plus those other problems he was having that nobody knew about because he never complained. Never. Oh, he was such a handsome man! And then they found the cancer and like *that,* she snapped her fingers, he was gone. That's when Donny, cleaning his gun, she said, had his accident. But the day Rita was married and I was confirmed, no one was dead yet, and Johnny said, Listen, Jeanie, you're a lucky girl, I can still dance! And around and around they went, the one who could polka all night, my dad said, the other with shrapnel in his knee, shrapnel that swam like a fish.

Look, Rita's going after Pa! Grandma in her chair at the edge of the dance floor covers her mouth. She's been married forty-six years to a man their daughter is going after, to ask him to dance, and she covers her mouth in surprise and delight, like a little girl, because this will be something! Flanking her like sergeants-at-arms are Sophie and Helen, estimable women who know how to take charge and find children lost in a huge department store, and care for those who need care—they too at this moment are caught, made to blush and touch that blush with hands that have known work, hard work. And behind them, Johnny's Elsie and Joe's Jenny, quieter women than Sophie and Helen, not nearly as likely to say in public what's on their minds, but by no means women without opinions and voices—they also follow this drama of Rita crossing the dance floor all in the bloom of her day to ask Pa what's she's going to ask him, as if there were no word for it. None. Even Mary, a little apart from the others, is momentarily focused on this unusual event.

Nettie puts an arm around Mary and says something in Polish—something soothing, I think, for it sounds soothing—and Mary smiles at her. A smile that's funny, odd, because half is where it should be and half sinks back into her cheek as if there's not enough jaw to hold it up. Why haven't I noticed this before? Smiling like that, almost whispering, Mary says, Where have you been? and Nettie says, Fine, honey, I'm just fine. No, no, Mary says, wetting her lips, swallowing, *where* have you been? Oh, says Nettie, you know, busy, trying to get everything done. Mary looks at Grandma, at Sophie and Helen and the other women following Rita with their surprised and charmed expressions, and her eyes begin to water; she is still smiling—it's as if she can't stop smiling, even if her eyes are watering, even if it's difficult to hold up half the smile that's sinking into her cheek—and then she looks at me, wants my hands. I give them to her and she holds on tight as if I alone can help her, understand what she means.

I am ten years old, a recently confirmed Soldier of Christ, holding my aunt's hands and waiting, I guess, like the mute chorus of blushing women beside me, to see if Rita will be successful in getting Pa to dance. But my waiting, my curiosity, is nothing compared to theirs. Theirs is great, mine is small. It is only now, years later, that I am interested, so interested that I can hear the horns and accordions suddenly cease their bouncy polka and begin a waltz—"The Blue Danube"—which Grandma has told me was always his favorite.

I can see her eyes, like Mary's, water up, can see her work-roughened ruby fingers absently stroke her cheek. She is lost, I think, helpless and happy and sad all at once. She doesn't know where she is in this enormous swirl of time that God has given her—it's so confusing to *remember.* It's much easier in church—everything is much easier—because there she has her pew, the same one all these years, the same nicks and knots in the polished wood, the same altar, statues, candles, and the same Mass—no, not quite the same, the Latin is gone, but the priest talks from the pulpit in Polish and what she *feels* is the same.

"Grandpa?" she says, as if addressing him, calling to him softly across the room.

We are in her kitchen, at the big table where he ate his soup, said his rosary. He sat in the chair I am now sitting in, my back to the stove, my eyes, like Grandma's, on the picture on the far wall. It's a picture showing a small girl in a bonnet and long skirt leading three cows along the ridge of a field at dusk. It's milking time, and maybe afterward Grandpa will come into the house so she can feed him, and perhaps play for him on the piano his favorite waltz.

"Did you play 'The Blue Danube' for him?"

My grandmother's eyes close. When she opens them again she is looking at the red hands in her lap, where she turns round and round the gold wedding band on her third finger. The band is flawed, not a complete circle, because years before something happened to that hand, a bee stung her and the fingers began to swell—oh, she begged her husband not to do it, everything would be all right, but he cut the band anyway. And in her kitchen on the farm years after Rita's reception my grandmother gazes at the cut her husband made, and I am thinking that whatever else she might tell me about, "The Blue Danube" is lost, as lost as the space in her wedding ring.

Then, surprising me, surprising her too, a smile begins to form on her lips, girlish, and she touches it, covers it, glancing quickly around the room as if someone might catch her at being—what?—light-hearted? silly? Our eyes meet for a moment and I smile with her, and nod, as if to say *I know.* But I don't know anything except that smiling is okay, blushing too, she's entitled to either one, both. Then sighing, she says, "He was right."

"Grandpa?"

"Yes, Grandpa was right to cut my ring, and I was wrong to yell at him so." Again she sighs, deeply, as if a great weight has been lifted from her shoulders, and after a moment says, "I didn't always understand my husband."

A weight has been lifted from my shoulders, too. I am not here to quiz my grandmother, not here to cause discomfort by asking things about the past which are difficult or confusing to remember. This is only a simple visit; I am just passing by, not staying long. I tell her I have recently quit my job in the Upper Peninsula and am moving to Iowa. I tell her, after we finish our cake and coffee, that I have all these books to pack, a long drive, and I am standing up to give her a kiss when she tells me about his books, his reading, oh yes, in that chair. I know about Grandpa's fondness for reading, his lists, my mother's trips to the library in Detroit. But what I don't know as my grandmother takes a twenty dollar bill out of her purse is that even on his last day, she says, he had one in his hands. She thought maybe it was his prayer book. She thought maybe he knew his time had come and he took his prayer book outside to have it close. She is folding the twenty in half and again in half, to make it less conspicuous. I ask if she has that book he was holding. She says she wants to give me a little something for the trip. Was it his prayer book? I ask. No, she says, this Korzeniowski again, and she presses the small square of money against my chest, saying, Here, please, it's nothing.

Almost two decades after Steve Szostak was buried she was telling me—while pressing a folded twenty against my heart—that her husband died with a book by Joseph Conrad in his hands; telling me this not casually exactly, not by-the-way, but because my earlier comment about packing books reminded her of something, something that had been with her so long now it was part of her, and important certainly—because it was connected to Pa—but maybe not something many people would care to hear. She herself, I knew, was more interested at that moment in giving me twenty dollars to help with my journey.

I said, "Grandma, I would very much like to see that book."

She blushed. Her color and expression were a visual echo of the photograph hanging in my mother's guest room, of a young woman who had spent the afternoon in her flower garden, alone, thinking how lovely everything was, how temporary, and just at that moment when happiness and melancholy competed most for her heart, the photographer snapped her. Or so I judge now, writing this long after that day in my grandmother's kitchen when I asked to see the book her husband was found holding in a patch of hollyhocks and thistles.

The River

I called Lupe at Holy Redeemer. I called St. John Cantius, where Father Szczgiel told me his name meant "goldfinch" but everyone pronounced it "seagull." I tried St. Ann, Most Holy Trinity, All Saints, circling the area around Plumer and Junction like some kind of bird myself, a hawk, a buzzard. Nothing. No one could help me. Father Leo Reilly at St. Ann sounded especially disappointed—almost sad—that his books had no Szostaks, particularly no mention of the two children who, if they were never baptized, would be forever in Limbo, could never see God. He did not say this, but he did not have to say it. Though I was told it was closed now, all boarded up, I even tried St. Vincent de Paul—maybe in the spirit of its charitable namesake a line had been left open for beggars like me. For indeed I was beginning to feel like a beggar, a beggar with a buzzard's need to grasp something, tear it, maybe even open an old wound better left scarred shut. A somber recorded voice told me to contact the archdiocese.

First I gave some thought to Wyandotte, which lies directly south of Detroit on the Detroit River and where shipbuilding had long been conducted, even before the Civil War. If I wanted to find out whether my grandparents had been married in Wyandotte (or in Detroit), all I had to do was contact the Wayne County marriage license bureau. Why this meandering, less certain route of calling up churches? Because I wanted more than just a yes or no? Because I wanted to know about Karol/Stanley and Stanley—about Limbo—and a government office has nothing to say about children and Limbo? Or what?

Aunt Elsie, Johnny's widow, still lived in Wyandotte. Maybe she'd heard something about Steve and Nelly being married there, something she'd heard from Johnny, who'd heard it from somebody else, a remark no one had taken seriously, because wasn't it gospel in the family that Pa and Ma had been married at St. Hedwig's? Attended that parish all those years in Detroit, sent kids to school there? And besides—listen—what with all Pa's stories about the kings and queens of Poland, how was it possible for him to marry Ma anywhere else? St. Hedwig's was named for Poland's greatest queen! They'd heard about her a thousand times, no? How she'd been betrothed in her cradle to a German prince, but married instead—because how could she marry a German?—the Lithuanian, Jagiello. Jadwiga and Jagiello created a flowering in the land; and Poles from that time to now—for almost 600 years—have known that young, beautiful, intelligent Jadwiga was the principal architect. Fabulous Kraków, its illustrious university, Wawel Castle, the golden-domed church—and more!—all from her inspiration. She was beatified, of course, declared by the pope to be in heaven. So how could Pa not marry Ma in St. Hedwig's? But he didn't.

Therefore, Johnny might have heard a foolish story, about them being married elsewhere, and mentioned it to Elsie. Or not married at all, not by a priest anyway—essentially the same thing—because of some argument Pa had with somebody, you know the temper he had . . . and if Ma was pregnant with Karol/Stanley . . . and the baby died . . . unbaptized. . . .

My thoughts, like dust bolls, rolled around. In 1902 Joseph Conrad published *Heart of Darkness*, perhaps his deepest inquiry into the human heart, a story about—what's hidden? Apart? The soul? Charlie Marlow narrates this story—years after the events—on board a yawl, a jolly boat, called the *Nellie*. "Do you see the story?" he says to his listeners. "It seems to me I am trying to tell you a dream . . . No, it is impossible . . . to convey the life-sensation of any given epoch of one's existence—that which makes its truth, its meaning—its subtle and penetrating essence. It is impossible. We live, as we dream—alone. . . ."

And yet, Charlie Marlow continues telling his story. "The broadening waters flowed through a mob of wooded islands; you lost your way on that river as you would in a desert, and butted all day long against shoals, trying to find the channel, till you thought yourself bewitched and cut off for ever from everything you had known once—somewhere—far away—in another existence perhaps. There were moments when one's past came back to one, as it will sometimes when you have not a moment to spare to yourself; but it came in the shape of an unrestful and noisy dream, remembered with wonder amongst the overwhelming realities of this strange world of plants, and water, and silence. And this stillness of life did not in the least resemble a peace. It was the stillness of an implacable force brooding over an inscrutable intention. It looked at you with a vengeful aspect. I got used to it afterwards; I did not see it any more; I had no time. I had to keep guessing at the channel; I had to discern, mostly by inspiration, the signs of hidden banks; I watched for sunken stones; I was learning to clap my teeth smartly before my heart flew out, when I shaved by a fluke some infernal sly old snag that would have ripped the life out of the tin-pot steamboat and drowned all the pilgrims; I had to keep a look-out for the signs of dead wood we could cut up in the night for next day's steaming. When you have to attend to things of that sort, to mere incidents of the surface, the reality—the reality, I tell you—fades. The inner truth is hidden—luckily, luckily. But I felt it all the same. . . ."

I dialed Elsie's number. "Such a long time!" she said. Yes, yes, she was fine, fine, the kids too. Johnny was a commercial fisherman out in California, in El Granada, he had *two* big boats now, and Elaine ran a bingo game there in Wyandotte. "I help her out so I don't become stiff!"

Ticks of static on the line got in our way. She thought I wanted to know where she and Johnny got married. "November 29, 1941, right here in Wyandotte. . . ." The day after his dad's birthday and two days after his mother's, I thought. "Oh yes, we were married practically on the day the war began . . . at six a.m. in St. Joseph's Church . . . a small wedding . . . just our witnesses . . . eight days before Pearl Harbor . . . and six months later Johnny went overseas. . . ."

There was more and it swirled into that large romance about young men and their sweethearts getting quickly married, pledging their small holdings in a world bent on pulling them apart, maybe blowing them up, the men in uniform, the women in knee-length dresses and hats with nets, the ministers half-asleep in their nightshirts, the best man and maid of honor a couple they met maybe five minutes before, the honeymoon in a borrowed room, under a tree, beside a lake, anywhere. But my mother wanted into this story, too, dancing for three days in her orchard. And I wanted in, racing around a hayfield with Grandpa, singing "Gee!" and "Haw!" Donny too was in motion, lining up bowling pins, cleaning his hunting rifle. Passion, fire, scars, dream houses, and Nelly Szostak slipping a book under her husband's arm just before Mr. Savage closed the lid. The facts and memories of our lives—how they can hound us into chasing after them, that we might catch and shape them into a visible, composed, embraceable thing.

I called Roman Godzak, archivist for the Archdiocese of Detroit. Yes, he had marriage and baptism records and would be happy to help me—but the records were filed by parish. I would be helping him, he said, if we could begin with a parish.

So I continued calling around. Angie at Our Lady of Mt. Carmel (1899) in Wyandotte apologized for taking three days—"but those early records are in Latin and Polish and I had to corner Father Redwick to translate them for me. Gee," she said, "I was really hoping I'd bring you luck, my name being Angeline too."

My list was growing shorter. Of the nine Polish parishes established in the archdiocese in 1902, four could find none of my Szostaks, St. Stephen's only kept records since 1920, St. Albertus, St. Casimir, and St. Stanislaus were closed, and Sweetest Heart of Mary—founded the year of my grandmother's birth—was still looking.

In the evenings I read Conrad. For clues to my grandfather? I actually heard myself bleat this out one night: "Look at all they had in common!" Both were adolescents in the Austrian-occupied part of Poland, and fled the country as teenagers. Both were sixty-six when they died—in English-speaking countries—

in August—of heart attacks. Their birthdays were within a week of each other (Steve's on November 27, Conrad's on December 3); both were Sagittarians, born under the sign of The Archer. (I even looked in that day's newspaper for their horoscope reading: "Tempers may flare, but at least the conflict is out in the open.") Both men had famous tempers. Each one named his last son John (Steve named his next-to-last Joseph) and each man late in life created a woman named Rita: my grandfather literally, Conrad in literature—Rita de Lastaola, a peasant girl who finds great riches and the virtuous gun-running George in *The Arrow of Gold,* a lesser novel written in 1919 when Conrad was sixty-two, his powers waning. At sixty-two, my grandfather one day was standing beside Rita when Aunt Sophie snapped his picture and caught him looking puzzled.

Both men were dreamers—their biggest connection. In their forties they abandoned large industrial cities to live in the country. Conrad left London for Pent Farm (but to husband his memories and sentences, not the soil) and Steve left Detroit for land he didn't intend to farm that hard. For wives, they both chose women who provided domestic comfort and stability—Jessie and Nelly—simple women who were not readers and who learned to stand back when the brooding began. "How little I really knew of the man I married," said one. "I didn't always understand my husband," said the other. Though Roman Catholics, Conrad and Jessie were married in a civil ceremony. Were Steve and Nelly also married outside the church?

Well, write to the Wayne County Clerk, for God's sake!

Why did I resist doing that? Because my mother told me to "leave us be"? Because I would learn what I'd begun to suspect? Hell, I was already probing the family's past, sticking my nose in, my claws—what difference did it make whether I queried Father Szczgiel or a nameless county clerk? As for baptisms, yes, a church was the source for that information, but I could get it, or try to, separately. No matter where Steve and Nelly were married, they still could have had those first two children baptized.

So, no, it didn't make any difference whom you asked about the fact of a marriage, priest or clerk . . . unless, maybe, you were the son of a woman who put the bishop first, dancing second . . . unless you were the grandson of a woman who every time she accidentally dropped a piece of bread on the floor, fervently kissed it before throwing it away. Bread—the staff of life—the stuff the Communion wafer is made of—Christ.

To Nelly Szostak He was everywhere, watching, a stern presence. She really preferred the babe in His mother's arms, the story of Christmas. Good Friday was a terrible time for her. Even her arthritic leg, painfully bowed, hurt more that day than any other, she said. And if she dreamt about Him on the cross, she woke as if with stones pressing her heart. Most dreams were hard for her, even one as sweet and bucolic—to my ears—as an orchard fuzzy with new buds. I said, "Why, that's a very nice thing to dream about, Grandma." I was in high school, breezing through life, giving my visiting grandmother a few minutes one morning—

"Yes, but nobody was there," she said.

"The bees were," I said, and she looked away, embarrassed—I thought then—for having revealed something silly that made me smile. But now I know differently—know that the dream held possibilities for terror: being alone with it, stung, her husband gone. Where was he? Dead, yes, but where dead? There were finally only two places, heaven or hell.

My grandmother feared the unknown. She wanted assurances, days saved from Purgatory, a spiritual—and temporal—insurance. She wanted nothing to do with scenic views of deep river cuts when we drove to Traverse City to see Aunt Mary. She did not want to leave Detroit, did not want to leave the farm, did not ever want to miss Mass. She wanted to collect her sons' pay, feed her chickens, gather eggs, wring the necks of roosters when company came. And take Communion.

Yes, but—

When Steve took her walking in the orchard under those new buds, wasn't everything different? The sweet hum of starting fresh, the honeyed pauses between sighs. And what he told her! Wasn't it simple and rich as a blossom beginning to unfold? He was a boy, a man, he was Chopin's heart brought back home. He was brooding but not angry, he was in Wawel Castle where the poet Mickiewicz lay. Where plump, pink-limbed angels flew above the beds in which the kings and queens of Poland lay. . . .

And when Steve, down at the creek, bathed his bright shoulders under the alder shadows while she waited, what were Nelly's thoughts then? For in the summer of 1928, their first on the farm, before the country went bust, surely my grandmother joined him there. To wash her hair. To listen to the water falling over the stones by the bridge and think it was like the sound of hands clapping in the distance. Approving of them. Surely she felt better now about leaving Detroit. Where he'd been hurt. Where, when the terrible thing happened, she crawled under the table and was found there, by my mother, bawling. Yes, of course she went with him down to the creek, and drying her hair on the bank in the sun she *had* to feel better. Light-headed, a little delirious, even shy when hearing, suddenly, the joyous outburst of the orchard oriole—*what-cheer! wheer!* And though the song startled her at first—was someone watching?—she composed a little prayer of gratitude for being right where she was, away from the noise of the city, the confusion, the danger. And thanks be to God, they were both healthy. Perhaps—she might have blushed—too healthy. Oh, it all made her pleasantly dizzy!

In May of 1929 Rita was conceived. What were Nelly's thoughts? That Helen, Nettie, Joe, and John had also been conceived in the spring? That spring was hers and Steve's season—nature's way—God's plan—that she and her husband were indeed starting out fresh? That those stories he told about the kings and poets were responsible? My God, she was already twice a grandmother with Stanley's Gabe and Helen's Leonard, and Nettie, that headstrong girl, had hers on the way too. She would be forty-four, Steve forty-eight when this one was born . . . almost ten years after John!

Beside the house that spring, in a sunny plot, Nelly planted her garden. She planted good things for her soups, her pierogi, her canning jars—like beets and onions and cabbage—and good things just to look at and smell, roses and jonquils, irises, peonies. She planted parsley and dill, strawberries and kale and tomatoes. And in the shade she planted lilies of the valley. Steve turned over the earth, young Joe and John scattered manure. Andy, up from the city in his Rickenbacker, helped out too, giving advice, my mother said. "He was always good at that—and bringing us treats." No doubt contributing dollars as well, for in the spring and summer of 1929—almost right up to the Crash—Andy was back operating a press in The Rouge's steel room, making big money. And telling how the country was growing, busting its britches it was growing so fast. In fact, on his next visit he was bringing them a car. A nice Model T.

So in the summer of 1929, despite moments of uncertainty, of lassitude and confusion, Nelly Szostak must have felt very rich. No, no, not money-rich. Rich in all those *other* ways . . . ways that made her blush. She was producing again, her garden, flowers, a child . . . and look at her husband—look at him!

In the summer and early fall of 1929, before the Crash, she would secretly watch this man. From a window, from behind a tree, when he read his books. Even at night, after he'd gone to bed, she would quietly climb the stairs and see him there, in his corner under the moon, all covered up like a bear. Watch him and wonder who he was, what he was thinking *now* (just as I did later!), and then—who knows how long she stood there?—long enough to remember his story about the graves in Poland, how millet and poppy seeds were scattered on them for when the dead returned as birds?—and then she went back down the stairs, to her own room, to her thoughts of this baby, this gift, this forgiveness blossoming beside her heart.

How do I know all this? I don't know all of it, but having been told, over and over, to watch and *see,* I am trying to see. How quickly—when telling me about the Polish graves, those bits of millet—she made the sign of the cross, passing from robust cheerfulness to heavy silence . . . "an astonishingly vital people," the poet Milosz says of the Slavs, "who sink easily into moronic apathy. . . ."

My poor grandmother. One moment I present her returning to the sweet hum of freshness, the next moment she is practically beside herself with gloom. She is taken by her husband to the castle, made rich by his crooning song, and then all around them—in golden October, the season of harvest—men are suddenly jumping out of tall buildings, shooting themselves, the Devil is loose from hell . . . and in the orchard, where he had whispered so softly, a bee puts poison in her hand. Mother of God, that was the terrible blow—that sting—having her ring cut off—memories of losing Karol/Stanley and Stella come back—everything. And yet, out of this gloom a few months later, Nelly Szostak gave birth to her sunniest child.

And in a dream during my search for the church in which my grandparents might have been married, a talking seagull approached me and explained with bright eyes that they had found a friendly skipper who would tie the knot aboard his boat. "Call the Detroit River," the seagull said.

Hail Columbia

On 7 July 1902, a young woman whose name has not come down to us smashed a bottle of French champagne against the steel hull of the magnificent four-decker excursion boat *Columbia,* and on the main deck dance floor a band played "Hail, Hail the Gang's All Here!" Then the *Columbia,* painted a brilliant white, left the dock at West Jefferson and Clark Avenues in Detroit and began her maiden voyage, a ninety-minute trip down the river.

During the time the *Columbia* was being built—by the Detroit Shipbuilding Company of Wyandotte—Steve Szostak apparently lived in Wyandotte, whose large ethnic population—maybe forty percent of the total—was Polish. Is it too romantic to suppose this Polish blacksmith had a hand in her construction? Is it too romantic to imagine him, say, on a fine Sunday in 1901, boarding the interurban for Detroit and calling on Angeline Mysliwiec at her parents' house on Merritt and escorting her one block east to Clark Avenue and then a dozen blocks down Clark to the river? And there, at the dock, gesturing toward Wyandotte, wanting to explain what he did with fire and tongs, with hammer and steel? If Stefan Szostak, nineteen, a young Heraclitus with Slavic fire in his heart, steel in his hands, and a pretty Polish-American girl on his arm—if he was helping the magnificent *Columbia* rise, surely he would have mentioned it. Surely this son of Polonia, of a land alive in romance if not on a map drawn up by the conquering maniacs of Russia, Prussia, and Austria—surely by his few halting words, their tone, this countryman of Mickiewicz would be trying to say to the girl he had passion and dreams as large as the *Columbia*. Why else was he in America?

The simplicity of it! The beauty! This youthful, foolish, inevitable, necessary union. Look at them, nineteen and fifteen, the one all buttoned up in his immigrant's dark heavy suit, serious, proud, fearless, afraid—and the other in her first bloom, barely out of her mother's arms, also afraid, but her cheeks, she can't help it, inflamed. And what's in store for them? Where in God's name are they going? East, west, north, or into the poor blackened pot of cabbage-smelling soup? They are going, on this fine Sunday in 1901, upriver on a ferry, toward Belle Isle Park, and en route he is searching for a way to say what he knows of the world.

And what is that knowledge he carries? The knowledge that makes him wave his arms, strike his breast, gaze at the water? And say her name—her Polish name, Aniela—in a voice more loud than he intends? He draws an almost painful breath, reaching deep into his lungs for a calmer approach to those things he knows, has seen and felt and fled—yes, fled—soared from like an eagle, a hawk—draws a breath and says to this girl, softly, while still gazing at the river below, "Aniela. Aniela Mysliwiec. . . ."

The difficulty is he has too much to say, and when he opens his mouth it all wants to pour out at once! There is the great *Columbia,* of course, whose brass propeller alone is eleven feet across and weighs almost three tons—a boat capable of taking on 3,000 passengers, more than any ocean liner—and he, a simple immigrant, is helping to build it! But when he thinks of himself as an immigrant, he can't help remembering the monumental poverty of his town, his region, the worst in Poland. And of course there is no Poland—and he fled. Like a great, fearless bird? No, like a crow, his belly full of stones.

Meanwhile, the face of the girl beside him is radiant. Oh, if they were in Poland he would take her hunting mushrooms in the Białowieska forest—for she has a face that belongs there, a face among ferns, a fresh, earthy, shy brightness among tall trees—or he would take her south, to Zakopane, the Tatra Mountains, for it is that kind of face too! Full of sky! My God, he is dreaming, and here is his heart, now in his breast, raging, and now in his mouth.

My poor grandfather, nineteen, wrapped up tight in his immigrant's coarse heavy wool, proud, masculine, and utterly unable now to say one word beyond her name all the way to Belle Isle.

There, walking under the trees, among the strolling couples, the situation is worse. What a mistake to come here! With this American girl! She—look at her, averting her eyes, sighing—she cares nothing for him! And why should she? He is no one, an immigrant, an ignorant blacksmith from the most miserable part of Poland—which doesn't even exist! If he turned around then, took her back home, in a week—no, in a day, an hour—she would forget all about him.

My grandfather's heart has left his mouth, abandoned his breast, disappeared. He is as good as dead. And yet the words and laughter from the passing couples—the rich, confident Americans—reach his ears, so maybe he is not completely dead.

Also reaching his ears—from inside, slowly, and then powerfully—are some other words. Polish words. From the beloved Mickiewicz, yes, to his beautiful Maryla . . . penned before he was sent into exile, away from her—

> "Precz z moich oczu!" posłucham od razu.
> "Precz z mego serca!" I ono posłucha.
> "Precz z mej pamięći!" Nie, tego rozkazu
> Moja ni Twoja pamięći nie posłucha.
>
> ("Go away from my eyes!" I would instantly obey.
> "Go away from my heart!" Even my heart would obey.
> "Go away from my memory!" No that command
> Neither my memory nor yours will obey.)

Stefan Szostak is rejuvenated. His heart comes back—how can it not in the presence of Mickiewicz!—but at the same time it is on the verge of breaking into God knows how many pieces. That was how it was with the poet, and that is how it is now with Stefan Szostak, nineteen, walking beside this American girl who does not look at him and sighs with boredom.

He and Mickiewicz are one.

So he must leave her. Must leave those hard eyes, that white neck, those little feet. Tomorrow—to her—it will be as if this day never happened.

Too bad they are not playing chess! In the poem Mickiewicz and Maryla are playing, and when he declares his love for her he points to the pieces on the board, their arrangement, and says that in the future, whenever she sees that arrangement, that captured moment, she will think of him.

Na każdym miejscu i o każdej dobie
Gdziem z Tobą płakał, gdziem się z Tobą bawił,
Zawsze i wszedzie będę ja przy tobie,
Bom wszędzie cząstkę mej duszy zostawił.

(In every place and in every moment
Where I was crying with you, where I was playing with you,
Always and everywhere I will remain by your side,
Because everywhere I have left a particle of my soul.)

On Belle Isle on a fine Sunday in 1901, among young couples strolling under the white birch and silver maples, among old men in dark coats playing chess, their boards and hands speckled with sunlight and leaf shadow, in this tranquil setting whose harshest sound is that of a soaring waterbird, Stefan Szostak, nineteen, a proud immigrant, a man in love and in doubt, is fighting with himself. How can he possibly think that Aniela Mysliewiec is bored? How can he possibly consider—after all week dreaming of her, of this day—how can he suddenly consider fleeing from her side, her life? Easy—it is in the Szostak blood to take off. When unhappy, stuck, in doubt, in love—hit the road, the ocean, grab a horse, fly! Does he have to be Chopin to flee? Mickiewicz? Does he have to be a Polish romantic poet—a Słowacki, a Lenartowicz—to run to Paris, Rome, Florence, the Levant—to die in flight and be buried away from home, forever in exile, in Limbo? (Stefan Szostak in 1901 doesn't know of course that these exiles will later be brought home for reburial—and with great honor—but if he did know, his loneliness at this moment might be even worse.)

He is sinking, and knowing what happens to Mickiewicz' Maryla (she married another, married rich, a count!), and knowing what happens to Słowacki's great first love, Ludwika

Sniadecki, who is everywhere in his poems (she preferred a Russian!), my poor grandfather is sinking fast. Under the weight of Polish history, which is a history of losses, of gloom, my grandfather even considers, I think, running away—like his brother Jakob—into the church. Why not? Only into a severe, silent monastery. He would wear a hairshirt, meditate all day, and at night sleep on the ground. What difference did it make that Maryla later regretted not marrying the penniless poet? What good are regrets when your heart is broken into a thousand pieces, one for each year of Poland's sad history?

Oh hell, this effete whiner isn't my grandfather! I saw him hammer hot steel, repair anything that was broken, I saw him take a bull by the head and almost rip the ring from its nose!

But you also saw him sit for hours in his orchard gazing at the sky . . . saw him kneel down and press his forehead against the bull and whisper to it, practically croon his heart out. And you know how sensitive the Szostaks are to slight, real or imagined. Remember in West Branch how your mother pulled her hair and yelled at the ceiling when she heard *Shoe Stack?* Remember how fiercely she wanted to leave that town—and did?

I know. My mother and her father and Adam Mickiewicz are one. . . .

So here is Stefan Szostak, nineteen, in Belle Isle Park in Detroit on a fine Sunday with Aniela Mysliwiec, shouldering, holding in his heart, a history of oppression, of flight, of pride . . . and the ghost—no, the living words—of a poet whose country, as Conrad will say, "demands to be loved as no other country has ever been loved . . . with the unextinguishable fire of a hopeless passion. . . ." Shouldering all of it—and at the same time, because of where he is *now,* in this new country he is eager to embrace, which includes of course the girl, he wants to express himself, his soul.

This is complicated, but I am trying to get to know my grandfather. A man in love may not be trustworthy—he is capable of saying or doing almost anything—but when is he more visible?

I am sure, in his immigrant's heavy wool, in his frustration, Stefan Szostak is sweating.

"Please," this shy voice beside him suddenly says, "take off your coat."

He is astounded, weakened by her concern, and in a few seconds those thoughts of a monastery, a hairshirt, sleeping on the ground—they fly, are dismissed as if so much nonsense. He feels better now. Feels better than better. Feels accepted! And of course he will ask this Polish-American girl, whose shy brightness belongs among tall trees—like these white birch!—he will ask her to marry him. He will ask her—and the thought comes rushing forward as a powerful, sleek, magnificent stallion might come out of those white trees—he will ask her to marry him aboard the great American boat he is helping to build, the *Columbia*.

The *Columbia*'s destination on her maiden voyage in 1902—Bois Blanc Island—possessed a well-known history that would have had a particular call, perhaps equal to that of the boat itself, on my romantic grandfather. During the American Civil War runaway slaves hid out in its woods. During the War of 1812 handsome, articulate Tecumseh, son of a Shawnee chief, held tribal meetings on the island, seeking ways to keep his people together and their hunting grounds free of whiskey-dealing thieves. The island was called Etiowiteedannenti, which meant "Peopled Island of White Woods Guarding the Entrance"—the entrance to the Detroit River from Lake Erie; and into this waterway came foreign nations to attack and capture the strategic and pretty place. It was the French who gave the island the name that my grandfather, almost a century later, privately must have practiced to himself . . . *Bois Blanc* . . . *Aniela* . . . as he tended the red- and white-hot fires of his heart, of history, and of the forge at the Detroit Shipbuilding Company, helping the *Columbia* rise.

But would my grandmother have consented to marry him aboard a boat?

No—absolutely not. She would marry him in Sweetest Heart of Mary, the Polish church I still hadn't heard from, that was looking in its files, that was founded in 1886, the year of Nelly's birth, in *that* church, yes, at the altar, not on a boat. Was this boat Catholic? Of course not. Or she would marry this passionate man in St. Stephen's, founded in 1874, good choice, perfect choice, his patron saint, the first martyr, the first of Christ's witnesses, stoned for speaking out, never mind that St. Stephen's only kept records from 1920—the archdiocese must have the earlier files. How can a church throw away forty-six years worth of marriages, baptisms, confirmations, and deaths? It can't.

Or if St. Stephen's is somehow not the church, there were three other possibilities—St. Albertus (1872), St. Casimir (1882), and St. Stanislaus (1898)—the three Polish parishes that had closed up, but whose records were in Roman Godzak's safekeeping. The archivist said he would search them out as the last resort.

So that's where I was with my grandmother shortly after she took my grandfather's hand in Detroit, in the brand new century, and said yes; she would marry him in one or another of these five Polish churches where you could hear Mass, smell the candles and flowers, and see the statue of the sweet Virgin holding her Baby and feel safe. Yes.

But—what about Aniela Mysliwiec? How would *she* feel? Would a shy, blushing, insecure, impressionable, sixteen-year-old Polish-American girl in love with a fiery, poetic son of Polonia—a man who had quoted Mickiewicz to her among the white birch on Belle Isle, from the deck of a ferry taking them toward their future—would she have thought about those words, his voice, his passion until all of her reason and training and fear evaporated like so much mist, until she was lost, lost as she'd never been, yet held too, enveloped, protected? Would she have trembled and wavered in the little world she had known until she was dizzy, dizzy, and finally willing, eager, to follow his? Beginning on board a magnificent four-decker excursion boat that he had helped build? And traveling, the two of them on *their* maiden voyage, to an island whose history, like Poland's, included the history of the hounded, the independent, the defeated, and the brave?

He told her such stories! About devotion, pride, faithfulness. About King Krak, who had a problem with a dragon. A big problem because this was a big dragon, and it was eating up everything it could get its mouth on. King Krak—the founder of Kraków—sent out word to all of his knights that he needed help. They came with swords, spears, and bows and arrows and tried to kill the dragon. One by one they all failed. All these big-shot knights were no good against the dragon, who by this time had eaten up almost half the kingdom. Finally a simple shepherd came forth and asked to try his luck. The knights ridiculed him, but King Krak, desperate, said for him to try. The shepherd built a fire, killed a sheep, and stuffed it with hot coals. He put the sheep near the dragon's den. When the dragon woke up, hungry, it ate the sheep in one greedy gulp. Immediately it needed water! Steam was pouring out of every hole in its head! The dragon ran to the Vistula and drank and drank until it blew up—like a balloon—and burst into a thousand pieces. Guess who became King Krak's greatest knight?

Aniela smiles. They both do. As my Aunt Rita will smile, years later, hearing such stories while pressing her cheek to the warm flanks of Jola and Sophie, Angel and Daisy, squeezing their teats, filling her pail, savoring the voice of her father. "Oh yes, he loved to tell stories when we milked, and they were almost always fabulous—you know, fables—with a moral. Pete and Jake were the same way—you couldn't stop them. You didn't *want* to stop them."

Still, look at her, at that face on the wall of my mother's guest room—a face, an expression, caught between happiness and melancholy, between Merritt Street in Detroit and the poets of Poland, between the Mother of God and a magnificent boat, between the known and the unknown, the safe and the dangerous—oh help her, please, these extremes are too great! She is only a simple soul who minds her parents and says her prayers—she is not some wicked girl in a book! Gary, why are you doing this to me? Please, write the archdiocese. Find out what's in those records. Hurry!

I wrote to the Wayne County Clerk. I learned that on 10 April 1902, Mr. Stephen Szostak and Miss Aniela Mysliwiec applied for and received a marriage license. He stated that he was twenty years of age, white, resided in Michigan, was born in Poland (to hell with Austria), by occupation was a blacksmith, and had not been previously married. He said his father was Anthony Szostak, that his mother's maiden name was Sophie Siepierska. Aniela Mysliwiec said she was eighteen, white, lived in Michigan, was born there, had no occupation, had never been married. She said her father's name was Andrew Mysliwiec; the space for her mother's maiden name was blank. The clerk duly put a line through the "consent" phrase at the bottom of the license because Aniela, by declaring she was eighteen, was therefore old enough to be legally married in Wayne County without a parent's permission.

Of course Aniela Mysliwiec was only sixteen.

Oh Grandma.

The Wayne County Clerk also sent me "a correct transcript" of the Certificate of Marriage between Mr. Stephen Szostak and Miss Angela Mysliwiec. It was filled out in his own flourishing script by the Rev. P. Gutowski—who declared he married this couple on 21 April 1902, in Detroit, in the presence of two witnesses, John Nichel and John Bos.

No maid of honor?

And where in Detroit did this wedding take place?

The Rev. Gutowski doesn't say.

Well, it didn't take place on board the *Columbia* the day she made her maiden voyage—7 July—so there goes that romantic notion. Stefan and Aniela either didn't want to wait that long—three months after getting their license—or had had no intention of marrying on a boat in the first place. Or they did have that intention, both of them—he *did* win her over to it—but something happened; something small and stupid and Stefan lost his temper. No, no, not at her—at that little man in the company office he had to go see for permission. And the little man in a bow tie, his oiled hair parted exactly down the middle, really was in favor of this request, oh absolutely, they could have their own minister or priest perform the ceremony too, everything would be just dandy! But then something happened. What? I don't know. Maybe the little man laughed—it was that simple—laughed in a way that Stefan's friends John Nichel and John Bos couldn't quite translate to Stephan's satisfaction, to his understanding of frontier humor, Yankee humor, entrepreneurial bow tie American humor, and my grandfather began to feel hot, feel insulted, ridiculed. And that was it. No boat. No goddamn boat. And he quit his job at the Detroit Shipbuilding Company of Wyandotte on top of it. To hell with them. He wanted nothing to do with them or their boat.

So no *Columbia*. It wasn't his idea anyway, never was probably. It's only my idea, my romance. Why? Because I've got boats on the brain, in the blood, like so many of Steve's other grandsons? Call Leonard in Florida or Ray at his home on Tamarack Lake near Ann Arbor, and they'll say: "Come down, come over, we'll go out in the boat!" My brother Greg has two homes—one down the street from my mother in Flint and one on board his 35-foot sailboat *Hennepin*. John, Jr., makes his living on fishing boats off the California coast. Jerry and Tommy, Nettie's sons, are probably on a boat in northern Minnesota right now, chasing mallards or walleyes or some smoky memories among the speckles of light on the wild rice paddies. Gabe most likely is about to sail off somewhere any minute, and Donny, of course, for years, could think of little else.

Maybe I wanted to connect my grandparents to the glittering *Columbia* for the same reason my mother embraces Alan Ladd and Robert Mitchum and Jean Harlow to describe her husband, her brother, and herself. We all wish to be among the stars, to shine, to go to Heaven in one way or another. Maybe I wanted to marry off this Polish couple on board the *Columbia* because it's so American—Hail, Columbia!—because I wanted them included in the country in a big way, because that's how we like things around here—and *now*—while the idea's hot.

I call Rita, tell what I've discovered. "Oh dear," she says, "then that's what it was, yes. I mean for years, all her life, Ma worried about that. She told us she said something when she and Pa were married that wasn't quite true. But she never hid from *us* she was sixteen at the time. Poor Ma, she'd feel terrible, you know, if people thought she had lied."

On 10 April 1902, in the Wayne County Clerk's office, Aniela lied. Because she wanted a license, and maybe Mr. and Mrs. Mysliwiec had said *nie, nie,* no, no, she was too young, don't be foolish. Or maybe her youth didn't bother them so much as her plan, hers and Stefan's, to marry aboard that—yes, bring it back—that boat! Just because they didn't wait until 7 July doesn't mean they hadn't planned on that date. Look how close it is to our nation's birthday. I still like this idea. I like it because it's romantic and foolish and on the brink, at any moment, of disaster. And there was a disaster—that stupid business with the laughing little man in the bow tie whose oiled hair was creased straight down the middle. Who in the grip of passion and history *wouldn't* feel insulted by such a man?

Yes, this was the plan—the great *Columbia* and Bois Blanc Island—and the reason that Aniela said she was eighteen. And even when the plan fails as it does, they can produce—thank God!—a better one; can still take a boat to an island, a ferry upriver to Belle Isle, and they can do this in the richest part of spring! Lent is over, Good Friday is over, Christ has risen again, the ice is gone, the trees are a soft green gauze of new leaves, and with Stefan's good friends John Nichel and John Bos and with Father Gutowski too, of course—that generous expansive man who calls her Angela—they can go to this place which is worlds better than Bois Banc Island!

Oh yes, I can see you blushing, Grandma—and no matter what else happened, not even the lowest, darkest, most unhappy moment could have made you sorry, either one of you, or let you forget. This is how it all started, in the spring of the year, and it, your life together, went straight through until Mr. Savage, standing beside the casket, asked if there was anything else. And remembering back to the words, to the passion, you said yes. It began right here among the white birch on pretty Belle Isle, because he took off his coat and held your hand and said poetry written by a great son of Polonia. And because after this idea, Grandma, I don't have another one. Not anything good. To tell the truth I have only some hurry-up affair pushed on you by necessity, by fickle nature, by a hard fact that you would not or could not reveal to your parents—

Gary, Gary, why are you talking like this?

Because you said what you said, Grandma, and because both of your witnesses are men. Where is the maid of honor? The church? But don't worry Grandma, Belle Isle is okay. Better than okay!

It is not okay. Write to the archdiocese. Now.

The Old Country and the New

A letter from Sweetest Heart of Mary arrived.

"I have gone through three volumes of names for your family, but to no avail. Your grandparents were not married here, nor were your uncles baptized here. I don't know what else to tell you other than write to the Archives. Who knows, you might get lucky through them."

Lucky. A word I heard often growing up. On the Gildner side its meaning was generally easy to understand. You either caught some fish that day or you didn't. But on the Szostak side you had to be careful about this word: it could make quick turns, leave bruises. It could pull the rug out, the plug out, then walk off with a smirk or with total indifference. On the surface it could be playful, you could laugh at it—oh well, unlucky at cards, lucky in love! But deep down it could nag, confuse you, give you the blues.

Gary, Gary, please, the Archives!

Yes, Grandma, I sent my formal request. I also spoke to the archivist Roman Godzak again because I had a question about St. Albertus. Who was he? I could find St. Casimir and St. Stanislaus in various texts, but no Polish St. Albertus. While Mr. Godzak was searching the files of the churches named for these men, I told him I wanted to read up on their lives. (St. Stephen, the fourth saint possibly involved in this wedding mystery, was definitely not a Pole—see the Bible, *Acts* 6 and 7—and thus I didn't think anything about my family lay waiting in the early files of St. Stephen's church.) He directed me to the Polish American Archives in Orchard Lake, just north of Detroit. Orchard Lake, he said, could tell me about St. Albertus. He gave me the number.

I got Carol Baerman, the assistant archivist. Yes, she had quite a lot on St. Albertus—St. Wojciech Adalbertus, actually. It was all in Polish, though, could I read Polish? I asked her to send what she had. In passing I mentioned that I had driven through Orchard Lake many years ago, remembered how lovely that area was, and seemed to recall a Catholic high school nestled in the woods.

"We have three schools here," she said. "Saint Mary's Prep, Saint Mary's College, and of course the Polish seminary, Saints Cyril and Methodius. We are all related. We are also the last of those woods you remember—an island, so to speak, surrounded by, well, suburbia."

She told me a little bit about each school. The part about the seminary—that its main work was supplying priests for Polish parishes in Detroit, and that perhaps sixty percent of the seminarians came from Poland—I paid particular attention to.

"How long has the seminary been doing this?"

"It began in 1855."

Naturally I was recalling Gabe's comment about Jake being a Jesuit, wearing black all the time.

"These aren't Jesuits?" I asked Carol Baerman.

"No, no. Diocesan."

But Jake might have been a Jesuit teaching there, I thought—if, in fact, we had such a man in the family. *If* we had, wouldn't I have heard more about him? A Jesuit, my God, is someone to be proud of! Unless of course something went wrong. I asked Carol Baerman if she might have anything in her records about my great uncle Jakob Szostak.

A few days later I received an envelope packed with Xeroxed copies of original documents, letters, a biography of St. Wojciech Adalbertus—all in Polish. I got everything translated, and it led me back, for a moment, to musing a little more on the subject, the emotional texture, of lucky.

Lucky—being lucky—doing well. Hey, nice clothes, nice car, nice *house!* And in the nice house, a special room—like something on display in a big department store. A room that's new, neat, kept ready. You could even invite the nuns over on Saturday afternoon to watch Notre Dame play football on TV in such a room. If you had such a room. We didn't have such a room when we lived on Buder Street, but my mother got this idea one fall, actually my teacher Sister Macrina (who was crazy about the Fighting Irish) got this idea, or dropped a hint about it, or so my mother figured hearing me tell how much Sister loved the Fighting Irish and if they, the nuns, only had a TV in the convent for that one afternoon, which of course was impossible. My mother thought and thought and thought about it and finally extended the invitation through me, and Sister was absolutely delighted and hoped Mother Superior would allow it, just for that one afternoon. And so for a week my mother cleaned and polished and shopped and cooked and was nervous and suddenly very unhappy, depressed, blue, because no matter what she did we didn't have a nice room. We were all unhappy, even my father (though not about the living room—he thought it was fine), because Sister Macrina and a couple of other nuns were coming to a house, our house, that didn't have a nice front room to sit in and watch the Fighting Irish clinch, I believe, their national championship. Well, it didn't happen. Mother Superior nixed the idea. We could all breathe, and be happy again, in our own way, in our plain old house on Buder Street that didn't have what nice houses—and presumably what nice, lucky people—have.

Was St. Casimir lucky? And if so, can we, by associating ourselves with this second son of Poland's King Casimir IV, become lucky, too? He loved to read, pray, and meditate. He gave his money to the poor, wore a hairshirt. When the nobles of Hungary asked King Casimir to send this son to be their king, the youth, only fourteen, tried to obey his father but at the Hungarian frontier he turned around and headed home to Kraków. Furious, King Casimir sent him off to some gloomy castle to think about things. The youth studied and prayed and slept on cold ground, which is what he liked to do. No, he wouldn't marry a daughter of Emperor Frederick III, either. Celibacy—and reciting, frequently, a long Latin hymn called "*Omni die dic Mariae*" ("Daily, daily, sing to Mary")—is what he preferred. Not surprisingly, given his habits, he developed lung trouble and died at twenty-three. He took to his grave—serenely and cheerfully, we're told—a copy of that Latin hymn.

Was St. Stanislaus lucky? Well, he was Bishop of Kraków and he had a problem with King Boleslaus II—Boleslaus the Bold—whose dissolute ways the bishop had had enough of. He censured the king. The king promised to reform, then as much as spat in the prelate's face by kidnapping a noble's wife for his savage pleasure. Stanislaus excommunicated Boleslaus. Fuming, Boleslaus burst into the bishop's chapel while he was saying Mass and knifed him dead. Boleslaus fled to Hungary, Stanislaus was canonized.

Wojciech Adalbertus was Bishop of Prague. He went to Poland to convert the pagans of the tribe called Prusy (later to be called Prussian), and they murdered him and chopped up his body. King Boleslaus the Brave (who preceded Boleslaus the Bold by a couple of generations) negotiated with the Prusy pagans for Wojciech's remains. The price agreed upon was the prelate's weight, in gold. They placed his corpse on a scale. Wojciech Adalbertus was a very thin man, a true ascetic, you'd think achieving a balance would be easy, and yet more and more gold had to be called for, an amazing amount, until finally—as the story goes—an old woman in rags passing by tossed on the great pile of precious metal a common coin worth less than a penny. It balanced things, and the Poles got their first saint (even though he was a Czech).

Now the story takes a turn. The Czechs, who have no saint, are jealous and steal Wojciech's body. The Poles steal it back. This thievery of the reverenced relic continues, back and forth, back and forth, over the course of several centuries, it seems. At times both countries claim they have it. Poor Wojciech, perhaps he is not so lucky being made a saint. When will this stealing stop? We don't know. All we know is that today, according to the Poles, *most* of his body is in the Cathedral of St. Wojciech in Gniezno—the first capital of Poland—located near Poznań. And every year on the anniversary of his death, 23 April, a special Mass is celebrated in Gdańsk, the site of his murder.

If Aniela and Stefan were not married on tranquil Belle Isle among the white birch, if this necessary union was not made in a green place where you could feel the literal American spring and its lush promises on your skin but instead was made inside a church, a church named for a Polish saint, which one might it be? The one honoring a youth who preferred books and a hair-shirt to ruling a kingdom? The one whose patron, demanding virtue, got a knife through his heart? Or the one whose patron's poor remains are still not completely at rest?

Which would bless Aniela and Stefan the most? Bring them the best fortune? I know, Grandma, I know, it's unlucky, practically blasphemy, discussing the matter like this, but *I* still prefer Belle Isle, and romance, and poetry. I think, deep down, the whole family does—including you, Grandma—no matter where your wedding took place. For sure it wasn't St. Hedwig's. You could have set the record straight, but you didn't. Why not? I say the answer is blushing, heart-thumping, curlicued romance—which leads me to the other stuff in this envelope from Orchard Lake. The stuff about Jakob Szostak who, according to Gabe, was a Jesuit.

First, his Baptismal Certificate, which says he was born on 26 May 1873, in Ostrów, and baptized the next day. His mother was Sophia Siepierska Szostak, daughter of Jakob Siepierski, and his father was Antoni Szostak, son of Ignacy Szostak and Marianna Jakson Szostak. Well, well, it looks like Ignacy, the grandfather, married a Scot ("Jakson" is the Polish spelling of Jackson) or possibly a Swede. Now this is curious: Jakob's Baptismal Certificate is dated 13 December 1894, when he is twenty-one.

The next document in the envelope is his School Certificate, which is dated fifteen days later, on 28 December 1894. It says he successfully completed fourth grade that month, and now was entitled to pursue fifth. His final marks were "Satisfactory" in Polish, German, and Arithmetic; "Good" in Reading and Writing; "Very Good" in both Religion and Singing.

The school was in Ropczyce, a mile or so from tiny Ostrów. Jakob had no absences, we're told. The certificate is signed by the school director, Mr. Wierzchowski, and by its religious leader, the Reverend Miętus, but nothing appears in the space for the teacher's signature. Perhaps Jakob, twenty-one at the time, attended the school via a special arrangement and did not have to squeeze himself every day into a desk designed for eleven-year-old fourth graders. Perhaps he had to appear only on examination days. His brother Stefan had just turned twelve; perhaps they were in the fourth grade together—the one excelling in religion and singing, the other gazing out the window, west.

The next document from Orchard Lake is a letter of recommendation. Written on 1 December 1894, by Jan Kudowicz, director of the posh Hotel Europejski in Lwów, it says, "Mr. Jakob Szostak worked in my restaurant kitchen as an assistant cook from August 20 to December 1, 1894. During that time he proved himself to be hard-working, eager, and honest in executing his tasks, and at the same time he proved to be a moral, peaceful, and God-fearing man. I have let him go at this request."

Lwów, a major city, is 100 miles east of Ropczyce. Surely he did not commute to school that fall. After leaving the Hotel Europejski's employ on 1 December, did he rush back to Ropczyce and a special arrangement with the school and, singing his heart out (it's the Christmas season, too), acquire his certificate in four weeks?

He apparently had plans—plans calling for papers—because that December he also picked up that copy of his Baptismal Certificate, signed by the religious leader Miętus. (Father Miętus would later sign one more certificate for him—we'll get to that.) What were Jakob's plans? He asked the Hotel Europejski for a second copy of its letter of recommendation—this one in German—so maybe he had his eye on Vienna, Berlin.

In any event, his whereabouts for the next seven years are not noted. He reappears in February of 1901, as a cook again—this time in the Catholic Boys' School and Orphanage in

Oświęcim, a good hundred miles west of Ropczyce. (Some forty years later the world would know Oświęcim as Auschwitz.) Jakob stays at the Boys' School until the following February. He leaves with a letter from the director, the Reverend Emanuel Manasser (a French name), written in elegant Polish, though the translation is mundane: "Jakob Szostak for one year has performed here eagerly and faithfully his duties as a cook." He takes this letter back to Ropczyce, where that summer he works for Wladyslaw Bursztyn, seller of wines and spices.

Mr. Bursztyn gives him another letter for his collection (using a phrase the Reverend Manasser had used): "Jakob Szostak was with me from May 1 to July 2, 1902, and during his stay he worked eagerly and faithfully and moreover his moral behavior was fine."

Two months later Jakob—who is now twenty-nine—receives that third certificate to which Father Miętus affixed his hand.

CERTIFICATE OF MORALITY

The office of the village of Ostrów certifies that Jakob Szostak, Roman Catholic, unmarried, was born in 1873, son of Antoni and Zofia Szostak, belongs to the community of Ostrów, has a certain right in that community, and is honest, leads a moral life, has never been suspected of or punished for anything, and therefore deserves a certificate of morality, with official signatures and official stamps of the village office and the parish.

Jendrzej Szostak
Village Official
2 September 1902

The above stated certificate of morality is confirmed.

Rev. M. Miętus
3 September 1902

Another seven years go by. We don't know where Jakob spends them with his certificates and letters. Then in 1909, at the age of thirty-six, he is in Chicago. A letter written on 25 August 1911, by the Reverend Jan Kosinski, of that city, says, "Jakob Szostak was cooking for two years at the College of St. Stanislaus while I was there, and as a cook he was a total success, and moreover very economical and thrifty. But he had one weakness, namely, to the alcoholic beverage if there was an occasion for it. But now he's claiming that for a year he has exercised restraint, with the exception of a small glass of beer now and then." (So much for that Certificate of Morality.)

The final document in his curriculum vitae is a letter written on 23 September 1911, by the Reverend Buhaykowski, from SS. Cyrillus and Methodius Seminary, Orchard Lake, Michigan. It says, "I need a cook and if Mr. Szostak has the necessary qualifications I would be glad to have him."

And there he went and there he stayed, apparently until he retired. He may have dressed in black, no doubt he thought about things, and we know he liked to tell stories to his niece Rita—stories with a moral—which his nephew Stanley's boy, Gabriel, probably heard too. Perhaps these stories—and the Orchard Lake connection, the black clothes—gave Gabe the notion that Jake—then in his late fifties—was a priest. As Gabe got older and learned more about the church, about the Jesuits and their going forth, the significant role they played in Michigan history (Pere Marquette was a Jesuit), perhaps Gabe, by way of fancy, made Jake a Jesuit too. Hadn't *he* traveled a lot? Besides, Uncle Jake the Jesuit has a certain ring to it. And of course since Gabe's parents were more or less estranged from Steve and Nelly, maybe the youth didn't see all that much of Uncle Jake, and distance, estrangement, added to the romance, as it will. Maybe Jake himself contributed to the romance—on one or more of those occasions when his known weakness to the alcoholic beverage enriched his tongue. Who knows how things went? Perhaps Village Official Jendrzej Szostak, who signed his Certificate of Morality, was a relative and descended from an important line. Perhaps Jakob's grandmother, Marianna Jakson, was the daughter of a Scot who was a professional soldier, an officer who came adventuring to Poland like those sixteenth century Jesuits—perhaps she was even the daughter or granddaughter of a great . . . ah, you see how romance takes our heads toward the high, the large, the castle with its 10,000 blazing candles, the cathedral with even more!

Once upon a time, in Galicia, a man named Antoni considered his three eldest sons: Jakob who sang like an angel, Stefan who was often dreaming under an apple tree—or was so furious about something you could not speak to him—and Piotr, the luckless one, who, no matter how hard he tried to complete a task, would fail. Clearly Piotr was not the son to inherit his father's small farm. Nor was Jakob—with that voice everyone said he must enter the church. He would, Antoni decreed, he would, as soon as he earned a little money for the family. That left Stefan. Don't worry, he will outgrow this dreaming. Look how strong he is—like a bull!

But then something happens. Several things happen. What? Life—life happens! With all of its commonplace noises and tics that clash and tally until a notion, an opportunity, occurs. Like spring it changes the air, changes your breathing, everything. Maybe Jakob comes back from Lwów, from the posh Hotel Europejski and its cosmopolitan views, comes back to Ostrów with money for the family, yes, but also with talk, stories, ideas. Stefan hears them. Hears his brother sigh. Can you imagine that sigh? Its depth? Jakob is torn, divided between his father's decree and the world, and Stefan is dreaming. The dream grows, fills the heart. Stefan receives his fourth grade certificate and then his blacksmith training, but all the while he is looking more and more away from Galicia, away from that poverty, those Austrians who rule them—yes—toward 10,000 blazing candles.

So what do we know, Grandma? We know that Jakob, traveler and fabulist, was not a Jesuit and did not come to America with Stefan in the late 1890s. By the time he got here—to Michigan, in 1911—Stefan had been married nine years and had fathered five children, four of whom were living and growing up on one side with stories about kings and queens and poets and saints and on the other side with a powerful, bursting-rich, slick image of America which told them they needed to become just like all those other kids born over here.

The Old Country and the New. Boom. Siss . . . boom . . . bah.

But Gary, Gary, what do the *archives* say?

They say, Grandma, that you married Grandpa on 21 April 1902, in the church whose patron, despite his hairshirt and celibacy—or perhaps because of them—was the most romantic of the bunch; the one who gave away his money, read books, slept on the ground, and took to his grave a copy of "*Omni die dic Mariae.*"

Great Odds

So the wedding site is at last identified, the mystery—if that's the word—solved. Roman Godzak also found in St. Casimir's files the baptismal records of Karol and Stanley, so Limbo is no longer a question either. Neither is *illegitimus*. Karol was born almost exactly one year after the wedding—on 18 April 1903—and baptized the next day. Stanley was baptized on 15 May 1904, three days after he was born. All of this sacramental ceremony took place about eight blocks north and fifteen blocks east of Plumer and Junction, on Twenty-third Street, between Myrtle and Ash. Bordering Myrtle and Ash are Magnolia and Butternut, and beyond these are Poplar and Forest. So in a way my grandparents were married in a kind of woods after all—and in 1902 perhaps the streets named for this flora possessed literal examples of it that the young couple could walk among into their future, smelling hints of clove and walnut, laurel and blue gum, and avoiding—especially Aniela in her wispy veil—the clinging scaly spike of the catkin.

Before they go off, let's clear up that first baby's name. His Baptismal Certificate says it's Karol, not Stanley. Why would Gabe think it was Stanley? Because that's what he was told. Who told him? Most likely his father. How would his father get this idea? How else?—from one or both of the parents. Now why would Aniela or Stefan tell their second son Stanley that he carried the name of the first, dead son when in fact he didn't?

Maybe it was not a simple telling. Maybe it went something like this: in a deeply blue moment, still grieving, still feeling—guiltily—that loss of her firstborn, maybe Aniela without thinking said to young Stanley that he was given to them by God as a gift in exchange for that pure, beautiful baby who was now in Heaven with all the angels. What a good time they were having. Can you see them? Playing? Maybe she told him this more than once, holding him tight to her young breast, rocking, seeking relief, release, mixing up prayer for the dead baby's soul with sweet murmurings to the living boy in her arms from whom she needed consolation and comfort, saying his name over and over like a question, and he not quite understanding where Stanley really belonged, up there or down here, or worse, to *whom* the name Stanley belonged, to him or the other . . . how could he? the mother didn't even seem to understand . . . though by and by it began to occur to him as he looked around, making connections between things he could see and not see, that he was something like a new wick in the lamp when the other, the bright beautiful other, disappears.

Gabe says his father disappointed Nelly and Steve. He drank too much, they said. Did he drink too much because for years he had to compete with a pure, perfect brother who went almost directly from his mother's womb into Heaven? Stanley went somewhere too—or tried. Way too young he joined the Army. Nelly's mother, Grandma Mysliwiec, got him out. Then at nineteen, still living at home and handing over his pay, he announced he was getting married, going on his own; he could afford it, he was making good money, proud of that, and Nelly, who had rocked him in her arms and murmured his name—held him and held him!—threw that good money in his proud face, threw him out, feeling betrayed. And then there's that second Stanley Szostak who worked at The Rouge. Not the Stanley Szostak whose address in Ford's archives matched my uncle's address, but the man who said he lived on a street I can't find; the man who worked in the furnace room from 1916 to 1927 and who might well have been Steve using the name of the disappointing son who had replaced the one that was lost. Was Steve now replacing *him?*

"Complicated man," says Leonard. "It wasn't easy being a Szostak," says Gabe, whose father would change the spelling of his name to Shostak.

In 1916 Stanley was twelve and certainly old enough to begin disappointing his father; but this isn't Stanley's story, it's Steve's. Consider another event that might have prompted the man to use his son's name: the death, in the spring of 1915, of Stella; the loss Steve's wife could never get over; the loss that, in those first months, we can imagine kept her fixed on her knees in a pew whose waxy odor was the odor of casket wood and funeral candles, that kept her in bed, in a chair, in a woeful, unseeing daze at the stove until the church doors opened again and she could go back and continue from where she left off. But where was that? North, south, east, or at the bottom of that blackened pot of bitter black soup? Perhaps Steve, wanting to escape, escaped into the name of his son—the son who also wanted to escape. And perhaps six years later when the son, now eighteen, lied about his age so he could run to that factory, perhaps the two of them, two Stanley Szostaks, passed each other as any two workers in the wonder that was all things to all men passed each other, their eyes circled by rings of grease and dirt, their tongues mute, and their hearts, ah, what lay in those when they saw something familiar about the other? Or did that sound in their skulls, that echo of steel against steel—and the heat they felt gathering like a fist at the tops of their spines—occupy them?

In the spring of 1915 when her sister died, Mary was three years old and seeing the world, hearing it, through the gloom of her mother's grief. Did Nelly take the girl on her lap seeking release and comfort as she may have with Stanley? We don't know. We don't know anything about this time, or not much. Oh, we know what we read in the news; we know a German submarine sank the *Lusitania* and 128 Americans were lost; we know the public outcry, the talk; we know about that talk earlier in the year, that fabulous, historic, transcontinental conversation between New York and San Francisco, between Alexander Graham Bell and Thomas A. Watson—"Hello, Watson, Bell!" "Hello, Bell, Watson!"—because it was all written down, recorded for us so we'd know. But nothing was written down at 4759 Plumer. No one kept a diary. No one kept notes, Christmas cards, birthday cards, Valentines, old scribbles aimed at praising, winning, explaining, wounding—no one kept anything with those marks the hand makes to reveal what might be singing, struggling, burning in the heart.

Henry Ford kept a diary then. "Don't find fault," he wrote, "find a remedy. Anybody can complain." And in a not unrelated vein, Judge Henry S. Hulbert of the Detroit Juvenile Court made a speech that has also been preserved. Addressing a group of employers, he said that Americans were willing to keep their children in school until the age of sixteen, but that immigrant parents were not so willing.

"They rear large families," he said, "and they begin, without exception almost, in poverty, and rise through a gradually increasing line of prosperity to a point where the maximum number of their children are of the working age and at home in the family, and then as the children marry or go out the parents, as a rule, go down the poverty slide again. The children are kept in school only so long as the law compels them to be there. They then force them into work, and confiscate the entire wages, almost to the last cent, for the family support. They build largely on the commercial value of their children. . . ."

In late November or December of 1915, about six months after Stella's death, Nelly conceived her eighth child. She may have conceived it on her birthday, or on Steve's, or even on Christmas. Statisticians of human behavior tell us that more babies get made on December 25 than on any other day of the year—the Christian year I reckon they mean. In any case, the following September, 1916, my mother was born, the sixth Szostak child who would reach maturity. Ford that year produced and sold half a million Model Ts. He was ecstatic, some thought crazy because of the high five-dollar-a-day wage he was paying. Gen. John J. ("Black Jack") Pershing entered Mexico to pursue the crazy Pancho Villa, who had been raiding U.S. border areas, murdering American mining engineers. Villa got away, but Black Jack got in some good practice for the war with Germany coming up. A bomb exploded that year during the San Francisco Preparedness Day parade, killing ten. Tom Mooney, a labor organizer, and Warren Billings, a shoe worker, were convicted (but pardoned twenty-three years later). John Dewey, speaking out for reason in 1916, published *Democracy and*

Education, and Carl Sandburg, just speaking out, published his *Chicago Poems* ("Come and show me another city with lifted head singing so proud to be alive and coarse and strong and cunning. // Laughing the stormy, husky, brawling laughter of Youth, half-naked, sweating, proud to be Hog Butcher, Tool Maker, Stacker of Wheat, Player with Railroads and Freight Handler to the Nation.")

That wild year in which my mother was born her father was thirty-four and her mother thirty. Stanley was twelve, Helen ten, Andy nine, Nettie six, and Mary four. None of the Szostak children, according to St. Hedwig's, was in school. What were they doing? Already working, most of them, helping the family rise out of poverty, as Judge Hulbert suggests? And where was Steve? Was he—if we stretch things a little—somewhere in the Sandburg poem, proud and coarse and strong and cunning? Doing well? Acquiring another house? Standing on the porch, his whole presence possessing it, thumbs hooked in his vest? Was he a hog butcher, generous, sentimental, giving away half the profits, as my mother tells it? Was he already going down the poverty slide, walking home nights from Ternstedt's factory with his head low, meeting his daughter Nettie on the corner of Plumer and Junction, holding the hand she remembers him taking, looking so tired, so—oh, what's the word people use today to mean very tired? Or was he, as the Ford archives suggest, keeping the blaze in The Rouge furnace room red hot, husky, sweating, a man of thirty-four, yes, but bending his back like a twenty-eight-year-old, maybe even pulling two shifts, driven, almost mad to escape into something, escape from something, release from grief, from poverty, from a dream he'd had so long now it had gone flat and he could hardly bear to remember it sometimes, though in the quick slide of seasons he would see a piece of it when he least expected to, least wanted to, as when it appeared in that expression of pride, of fierce independence, in the face coming toward him, the face blackened by grease and dirt that could well be his own?

Six years have passed, passed like nothing, and that face he is seeing belongs to his son. Stanley is eighteen. My God, *he* was just eighteen, traveling on a boat with his loaf of bread to America, dreaming his dream, hammering steel, helping to build the great *Columbia!* And now Stanley is here, in The Rouge, making good money. And Helen, sixteen, is married to John Dobis the Lithuanian, who has $3,000 and will take care of her. And Andy and Nettie, fifteen and twelve, are in the sixth grade together at St. Hedwig's, though eager, chomping on the bit, to get out. Mary is ten and St. Hedwig's doesn't know where she is—does anybody?—but in body at least she is still at home with Jean, who is six, the two of them helping Nelly with this and that and with Joe, who is three, and John, who is one. "The language of facts, that are so often more enigmatic than the craftiest arrangement of words," Joseph Conrad declares in *Lord Jim,* a book about a man who is romantic, who is "one of us," who errs and errs and errs again trying to achieve grace, salvation—a book Steve Szostak may well be reading, wondering, like Jim, where *he* can find grace.

So six years have passed since that other Stanley Szostak began working in The Rouge furnace room—passed enigmatically and swiftly—and during that time a world war is fought to end all wars; 116,708 U.S. servicemen and women die in the war; the year it ends half a million Americans die from influenza (an estimated twenty million die worldwide); and no one in America is supposed to drink alcohol (not even Great Uncle Jake once in a while). During this same period a fictional town—Winesburg, Ohio—becomes famous for its quiet, desperate lives; a shoe worker, Nicola Sacco, and a fish peddler, Bartolomeo Vanzetti, are accused of killing two men in a Massachusetts payroll holdup, are accused of radical agitation and anarchy, and are executed seven years later—despite a worldwide campaign for their release on the grounds that the evidence is inconclusive and prejudiced. Groups advocating "hundred percent Americanism" rail and bray against Jews, Catholics, immigrants, blacks, reds; even Henry Ford gets around to blaming, in his book *The International Jew;* there are all these suspicions, accusations, riots, 300 men in Detroit are arrested on charges of—of what? being revolutionists?—held in jail for a week, denied food for twenty-four hours, finally found innocent of whatever it is they are supposed to be or have done. In the meantime President Wilson can't get the U.S. Senate to buy the League of Nations, an idea "to promote international cooperation and to achieve international peace and security"; he tours America, appealing to her citizens, and suffers a stroke; the citizens are being urged by the advertising boys to spend, acquire, get a car, an electric kitchen, put on lipstick, girls, smoke; the poet William Butler Yeats declares "The ceremony of innocence is drowned"; the poet T. S. Eliot believes "we are in rats' alley"; F. Scott Fitzgerald, ah, a breath of air, tells about fresh young men and women, about roadsters and necking and lipstick and illegal booze and America loves it, loves *This Side of Paradise,* loves him—or anyway a lot of people do—and he loves them back, desperately; Man O'War runs once around a track and wins $83,000; fleet-footed Jackie Robinson is born, and Sugar Ray Robinson is born with those sweet, stinging hands; Knute Rockne begins coaching at Notre Dame, winning with his fiery tongue the hearts of boys, of nuns; the heart of Frederick Chopin is brought back to Poland from exile because the Poles have their country again; there is peace in the land, music; Nelly's sister Anna is married to Casimir Solak, who plays the violin, the French horn, though to earn his bread he is preparing yet another scaffold for his construction business; and a house I will later occupy is being built by immigrants, German masons, who throw stucco on the frame with their bare hands, that way the stuff will stick, last forever—but don't ask how they do it, don't even get too close to watch, because they'll stop, because this two-fisted technique is *their* secret, seems to be the message, go learn your own.

So what have we learned? Aniela and Stefan speak their vows in a church named for a youth who takes to his grave an ancient hymn; marry in a church attached to a romantic story that praises a pure and inward art. Marry properly. That the witnesses are both men is very unusual ("I've never seen this situation come up before," says Roman Godzak), but then the groom is an unusual man. Likes to have a drink with his horses, read books, gaze at the sky. He sounds like a poet, except he never writes anything down—that we know. Is he looking in the sky back to tiny Ostrów? Those guys from the old country were all alike, Leonard says. They all wanted to go back. Maybe in Poland two male witnesses at a wedding are not so unusual? All these little mysteries, these questions, that romantics, those loners, stir up in our soup.

I spread the map of Detroit on my desk and look west, toward the Catholic cemetery closest to St. Casimir's, Holy Cross. It is not far from 4759 Plumer. In fact it's exactly on the way to The Rouge, right across from General George S. Patton Park (which of course wasn't there in 1903).

I call Holy Cross and speak with Andy Walerski, the superintendent. He tells me Holy Cross goes back to 1867 and yes, it's the one St. Casimir's used. He also tells me it occupies thirty-nine acres and is the smallest Catholic cemetery in the city. I think that's just fine, what I'm after is small too.

"I'm looking for my uncle Karol and my aunt Stella," I say. I give him their dates.

"Let's see what we've got," he says.

I wait, wondering if there is a statue of General Patton in his park . . . a statue with a tank or a horse for him to ride on. I think of a romantic story—about the Polish cavalry in 1939 riding out on beautiful brushed mounts, with sabres raised, to meet Hitler's panzers and getting blown away.

"Okay," Andy Walerski returns to the phone. "I'm going through the Szostaks in my box here . . . here they are . . . Stephen, oh five, eight months twenty-seven days old . . . Angeline, oh six, one month four days old . . . Mary, oh six, twenty-three years old . . . Stanley, nineteen fifteen, one year fifteen days old. That's it. No Karol, no Stella."

For a long moment I wonder where I am. I can't believe the outrageous irony of that list of names.

"You still there?" Andy Walerski says.

"So no Karol or Stella."

"Now we had a fire in here back in oh one or oh two that destroyed some records," he says. "Maybe your uncle's card got burned."

"He died in oh three," I say.

"Maybe it was oh three, that fire," Andy Walerski says.

I think of tombstones and vaults and sod—all the stuff in a cemetery that's difficult if not impossible to ignite.

"I don't know what to tell you about your aunt except try Woodmere Cemetery," says Andy Walerski. "It's just across the park. It's pretty old, and they take Catholics."

I thank him and go for a walk. It's a nice day. Spring has arrived. You can smell it, and it smells like spring always does, bringing back pleasantly confused subtle whiffs of creek bank and hay and youth and green willow. Who isn't moved by spring? In the spring my grandparents were married, exactly a year later they lost their first baby, and on their thirteenth anniversary they lost another. They also lost, were estranged from, two more, Stanley and Mary, who were perhaps given, had thrust upon them, responsibilities they couldn't handle, didn't want to handle, or just didn't understand. Some things, of course, are not meant to be understood. Spring, for example. First love. God's ways. I don't understand how you could put in a box the names of all the Szostaks buried in a largely Polish cemetery in Detroit over the course of what?—125 years?—throw the box in a fire at some point, kick it out, dump out the names turned to ash, and then find, now, in the last decade of the twentieth century, that the four entries surviving are Stephen, Angeline, Stanley, and Mary. The odds against this particular combination occurring in a narrative about a man named Steve Szostak who is the husband of Angeline and the father of Stanley and Mary, the four of them, each in his and her own complicated way, grieving over the loss of Karol and Stella who are not only dead but whose records of that fact can't even be found—as if they were too pure, too rare, to leave *anything* behind—the odds against this particular combination, as I say, am trying to say, must be something.

By and by I call Woodmere Cemetery. No luck. I call Mount Olivet—the Catholic cemetery next closest to Plumer Street—and no luck there. I call Our Lady of Mount Carmel in Wyandotte, founded the year Lincoln was shot. It too had a fire, I'm told, in 1919, which destroyed the records of its first fifty-four years. That's it.

No, there's St. Hedwig's, the parish Steve and Nelly belonged to when Stella died. A record of her funeral service might be there. I call, am told to send a written request. While I'm typing it my thoughts, leaping, land on Stanley Kowalski in *A Streetcar Named Desire* bellowing out like a lost and lonely bull, "Stel-laaaaa!" Then they land on Stanley Shostak, also married to a Stella. I saw them when I was a boy, but I can't remember what they looked like.

I call Gabe. He's home.

"I was just wondering," I say, "if I could get a photo of your parents."

"I don't have any. When my mother got Alzheimer's she threw them all out. If the frames were nice, like that oval frame my dad's Army picture was in, she sold them."

"But you do have the Army picture?"

"Somehow it was saved. Maybe I'll reframe it."

I ask if I can get a copy of that picture. He says it's fragile, but he'll look into it.

After we hang up I don't think about anything for a while, empty frames maybe, and then I think no indeed, it wasn't easy being a Szostak. Still isn't.

A Flock of Small Birds

That April when Stefan married Aniela in St. Casimir's, just a few blocks away at 1120 West Forest Avenue, where he was born, Charles A. Lindbergh was celebrating his second month in this world. Twenty-five years later he took off for Paris, slim and handsome in his sleek little plane, and six months after he landed my grandparents took off, too, for northern Michigan, Steve in a truck with their worldly goods, Nelly in a Rickenbacker automobile with four—or five—of their kids. We're never sure about Mary.

We can be sure about Lindbergh, though. That's the house where he was born! Perhaps Andy, leading this caravan, has steered the Rickenbacker past Lucky Lindy's birthplace on purpose. Perhaps Andy, who is three days shy of twenty, even makes a gesture with his hand and an engine noise with his mouth—suggesting the flight of the Spirit of St. Louis over their heads, over the ocean, *vroom!*

"If he'd gone down in the drink, what then? But he didn't go down, did he?" Andy might be saying, implying that if Lindy could succeed, so could they—trying to distract his mother and his little sister Jean from their gloom. Joe and John are taking this move just fine. A farm—horses and woods—would appeal to strong young boys. Put more muscle on them! Yes, this is a good move because—

Because the city's going crazy, the Italian gangs, the Jewish, whiskey-running across the river, shootings, blind pigs—even the Poles in Hamtamck are mixing the stuff and selling it out of their cars on Joseph Campeau—bad business, dangerous, not good for kids to grow up around, he and Pa had talked about it, Ma knew, everybody knew, no? But Ma doesn't want to hear. How can the country be doing so well and be so crazy! she says. Ah, Ma.

So Andy leaves all that stuff alone. He turns off Forest Avenue, onto Woodward, and the Rickenbacker's northern course is set. A straight shot to Standish, he says, 150 miles. If they average twenty-five miles per hour, they'll arrive in six hours. They'll be "making good time," he says. I know he says this because "making good time" is an expression, a desire, a reality in Michigan history that came into its own with the horseless carriage and is so fixed in drivers that it's akin to breathing and eating and recreating their kind. And I reckon he whistles at Lingbergh's good time: 3,610 miles in thirty-three hours, or 110 miles per hour. More than four times their speed!

I also know that these figures mean zero to my mother—they have nothing to do with who she is. And who is she? She is a young girl gazing at the Public Library as they pass it, at the Institute of Arts—two beautiful white buildings, huge and clean. Palaces, Pa called them. Italian palaces. And they are! And she has been in them, not to study texts or to train her eye for paintings and sculpture, but to invent, become.

Farther along the avenue, at Grand Boulevard, she gazes toward the majestic Fisher Building rising up taller than anything she knows, and in whose cathedral-like lobbies she has bravely ventured and seen her image, in marble and stone—*hers,* Jean Szostak's—returned so richly, so elegantly, that she too has seemed beautiful and rich and elegant, seemed part of a fabulous story. Never mind that the Fisher Building will not open to the public until six months after this November journey. It *will* be available to her, and when it is she will place its rich reflections where she feels they belong.

In my mother's lap is a box of Animal Crackers. It's designed to look like a car in a P. T. Barnum circus train—it's colored red, yellow, blue—and inside are the sweets. You can nibble off the elephant's trunk, devour the lion in one bite. My mother, eleven years old, holds these sweet animals in her hands. Her siblings and Ma hold their own. They are a treat from Andy, who wants his passengers not to be gloomy. After all, it's Ma's birthday. Look, Ma, a string—you can carry your box like a purse! Does Andy know that this happy little box appeared in 1902? If he does, what an interesting set of facts to announce. That 1927 is the silver anniversary of Ma and Pa's wedding, of Lucky Lindy's birth, and of the invention of the Animal Crackers box!

I think Andy is more likely to say something related to Ma's birthday—something educational and American, because even though he has had only two years of formal schooling, he prides himself on his knowledge of the world acquired from experience and from reading in the popular press. "You know, the year Ma was born the Statue of Liberty was dedicated!" For a moment this might get Joe and John's attention (Ma and the Statue of Liberty?), but it would do little to charm my mother or Nelly—birthday or no—into a better mood. So most likely Andy focuses on the road, his Rickenbacker, making good time. Leaves them all to their separate thoughts around the jolly box of treats that was originally designed, in fact, to hang on a Christmas tree. Maybe some of them are already thinking about Christmas, for it is less than a month away—thinking about a tree, Mass, the big dinner, and who will not be there.

The estranged Stanley and his wife Stella and their son Gabriel, who is three, will not be there. Nettie, crazy about her Irishman, will not be there. Helen, pregnant, will probably be afraid to travel. Mary? We never know about Mary, and must pray for her. Andy we can count on. He will drive up in his Rickenbacker. There is always one son you can depend on, and in this family it's Andy. We can't decide anything until Andy gets here! I can remember such deference paid to my uncle. I even thought at one point that *he* was the father in my mother's family, that the man called Pa was really only someone who showed up briefly to pat small children on the head and then, when you looked again, was gone. That he is riding in a truck apart from the others on 28 November 1927 seems altogether fitting.

What are his thoughts? That today his wife is forty-one? That yesterday he turned forty-five? That in twenty-five years they have produced ten children, eight of whom are living, and four—or five—of that number are riding in the car up ahead? That thirty years ago he left his father's farm with the clothes on his back and a loaf of bread and since that time has been wanting to return and is now returning? That he has served his penance in the noisy graceless world, in burning Purgatory, received his scars, and is now going back, as close as he can, to whence he came? Before it's too late? Before his eyes like the weary eyes of the man of finance, the man of accounts, and the man of law—those men listening to Marlow tell his tale of the *Judea* and her wretched 600-ton cargo of burning coal that's trying to reach Bangkok—before his eyes, like theirs, fall to "looking still, looking always, looking anxiously for something out of life, that while it is expected is already gone—has passed unseen, in a sigh, in a flash—together with the youth, with the strength, with the romance of illusions?"

Monday, 28 November 1927, is a fact, and so is Joseph Conrad's story "Youth" and P.T. Barnum and the Animal Crackers box and the caravan taking a Polish-American family from Detroit to a farm 150 miles straight north. Prohibition is a fact, and the Purple Gang, and *This Side of Paradise,* and Charles A. Lindbergh's birthplace, and Ostrów, and Adam Mickiewicz' skull—but the thoughts of my grandfather on this day can no more be measured or weighed than the *Judea,* or the island of Patusan where Lord Jim ends up, or the black man's blood in *Heart of Darkness* that fills Marlow's shoes, and I know it. I know that Steve Szostak, water and bone, can be measured and weighed; I can take a shovel and dig him out and lay him on a scale—the same as with a book by Conrad—but still something will be missing. I can feel it, this missing thing, feel its light, passion, confusion, or mystery until I shake, sing, swoon, or go mad. But I can't measure it, and I know it.

I go for a walk in my measurable neighborhood, and then I dial my mother's number. No answer. I try an hour later, three hours later—still nothing. I call my brother Greg.

"Has she gone somewhere?"

"No, she's there."

"Maybe her phone's not working."

"It's working."

"Why doesn't she answer the damn thing?"

My brother laughs. "She's just like you when you don't want to talk to people. She unplugs it."

"How is she?"

"Keeping us on our toes, like always."

I tell him I'm coming to Flint at the end of April, to give a talk at Dom Polski about my baseball adventures in Poland. I also want to visit with Donny's wife, and walk around Grandpa's farm, and maybe go to Detroit too.

"Will you have time for a sail?"

"I hope so."

I know why my mother told me to leave the family be. I've known for years, but I never really felt it until I began trying to see her in 1927 when she was plucked out of her story and thrust into her father's. Who wants someone messing up her invention with *his* invention?

She finally answers.

"Guess who?"

"Oh boy," she sighs, "now what's the malarkey?"

I tell her I was just talking with Doug and Patty Warner. The Warners, who live in Flint, are friends of mine; Doug is an artist and Patty is a photographer and former fashion model—and Polish—and my mother is fond of them, of Doug's courtly manners, and of Patty's wacky wit and the raves she gives my mother's cooking. What we were just talking about, I tell her, was the beautiful picture of Grandma in her guest room.

"How do they know it's so beautiful?" she says.

"I told them."

"They should make up their own minds."

"That's why I'm calling."

"Suddenly a light goes on."

"They say they'll be happy to come out to the house and take the picture and make a copy for me. If it's okay with you."

"Anything else you need?"

"Not unless you can help me find Great Uncle Pete."

"Pete? Call Chicago, that's where his kids went, all of them."

"Did he ever live in Michigan?"

"Of course he lived in Michigan. He was a farmer up north, a beet farmer. Oh, he was a nice guy, Uncle Pete, and he did very well for himself. In fact he was rich. He had two handsome sons, Tony and Johnny, and this French girl—what was her name?—she was crazy about him."

"About who?"

"Johnny. But he died, poor fellow, nineteen or so, it was terrible. His sister Helen died young too, around sixteen, another shame, she was gorgeous. And then they had Hattie, who ran a beauty shop in Detroit. And Marian, she was there too, she put in a good word for me with the manager, which is how I got work at Kroger's bakery."

"What did you do?"

"I lied, said I was eighteen. Well, at fifteen I looked eighteen. I lied about my age at the Sterling elevator too, to get that miserable job picking beans with Mary. Oh hell, everybody lied a little bit about their ages then, you had to. But Pete, I loved that guy, we all did, he always brought us candy, told us stories. Just like Uncle Jake. They made us feel important. You should have been there. Here, write about this, Shakespeare: Jake had a farm by the seminary, and Wallace, an unfortunate fellow who was a little slow in the head, but nothing serious, worked for him and looked after him in his old age. Then when Jake died, the lawyer came to my dad and Pete and said that farm is yours, half and half. They said what about Wallace? What will happen to him? The lawyer didn't know, maybe the poor farm. The poor farm, there's a lawyer, heart of stone. Anyway, they said no, no, give Jake's farm to Wallace. That was my dad and Pete, always generous. Now what else do you need? I've got to get my jalopy tuned—it's missing. We go down the road like a case of hiccups."

Before we hang up, she says, "Tell Doug and Patty to come for lunch. I'll fix the pierogis she likes so much."

So I get a copy of the picture, of Aniela at sixteen wearing a rose in her hair and a rose on her breast, and I'm back where I started, more or less, almost a hundred years ago. O Youth, O 1902, O Romance and Fact! She looks as if she should be in school, in church, in a parlor full of girls chaperoned by a nun and listening to "*Omni die dic Mariae.*" Doug Warner told me that when he took the picture out of the frame it was almost burning it was so hot. He meant from age, from the combustion, the oxidation of time, but my ear also heard metaphor, the mystery and passion of union. Sacred *and* profane. I heard my grandmother worry about her wedding ring again, about her husband cutting it off her finger; I saw her furious in the hay field, cheeks on fire, while Grandpa and I galloped round and round her; and I saw us in her kitchen, years later, when she gazed at the door as if any second he might appear for his supper, his rosary, his whiskey, and the next pages of that book she had buried.

On the phone to Chicago, thanks to Information, I get Stanley Szostak, the last of great uncle Pete's fourteen children. We start with names, a flock of small birds on the line between us; some fly off and come back in different places; some fly off and circle in the distance; some fly off for good.

"No, no," Stanley says, "my dad only had two wives. And the first one, Mary, died very young. But here's how everything started; they all followed Jake to America."

"All?" I say.

"Well, first Jake, then Pete, then Steve. Jake was a priest in Detroit. Pete lived in Detroit too—owned a bakery and a tavern in Hamtramck. For some reason Alberta, Canada, gets his attention. But our mother, Katarzyna, won't go there with him, so after a while he comes back to Michigan and buys a farm up north, in Pinconning."

"When did he buy that farm?"

"Before I was born. Even before the First War it had to be."

"When was your dad born?"

"April twelve—I think 1880. He died right after the Second War, in 1947. April twelve."

"On his birthday?'

"No, no one's a twelve, one's a fourteen. Let me go find this box."

While waiting I recall a recent exchange with my ophthalmologist's secretary. I phoned to make an appointment. She asked how old I was now, and I couldn't remember. I had to figure it out with a pencil and paper.

Stanley returns. "Okay, I found this box the wife put together before she passed. Here's Pete's card. Born April 12, 1879. Died April 14, 1947. Buried in Pinconning, at St. Agnes."

"Two years before Steve died," I say.

"Both fast. The only way."

"Do you know when Jake died?"

"First. They all followed Jake."

Right.

Suddenly Stanley says, "Here's my oldest sister Katie's card. Born oh one, died 1990. Long life. And here—my goodness—is a bunch of old photos. Nice ones. Of weddings. You should see what the wife saved for me."

His voice is fading. He is slipping away, I'm thinking, into the dreamy past. I'm also thinking that if Pete had a daughter in 1901, *he* was the leader. Then Stanley says, "I just remembered a funny story. My dad went back to Alberta, to see about this land he'd bought there, and found that some nuns had built a convent on it."

"What did he do?"

"Oh, he just gave it to them," Stanley laughed.

A Stupendous Grave

On the last Friday in April I set out for Michigan. I took along the ceremonial sabre the Poles had given me for coaching the Warsaw baseball team (I planned to show it during my talk at Dom Polski), and I took the spectacular hand-colored photo of Uncle Stanley in his First World War uniform that Gabe had sent (which I planned to show my mother). Spectacular is the right word for it. My uncle, at sixteen, resides in a large oval garnished with a bald eagle and a rampant Stars and Stripes. He wears a high-crown, dimpled campaign hat, and the eagle, fierce of eye and sharp of beak and talon, wings outstretched, grips the oval just above the hat. Whoever colored

this photo gave my uncle full, almost bee-stung feminine red lips; but no one messed with his gaze—it is straight on, made of eagle stuff, brave and ready for anything or anybody, savage Hun or Polish parent. How much actual military training my uncle got during this rebellious run from Steve and Nelly is unknown; probably he got very little; probably this picture is the chief credential he acquired before his grandmother fetched him home.

Steve would not have fetched him home. After all, he himself went off at about the same age: let the boy learn something. Also, this was 1920 when my grandfather may well have been working in The Rouge furnace room, perhaps even pulling a double shift; he had seven kids now, including the new baby, Joe, born just as the Poles got their country back—and I can imagine him thinking hard about getting away, too, to some land up north, as Pete had . . . because if Pete could do it why couldn't he? . . . why was he killing himself? No, no, let the boy learn.

Driving to Michigan I thought of a son and a father both wanting to run away and live the identities they were trying to make—and then I thought of Donny, who also wanted to run away, get free—and did get free—and then came back and shot himself, my mother said, cleaning his deer rifle.

I crossed the Mississippi River. A month before, I phoned Donny's widow, Jan, and arranged a visit. She lived in Au Gres, near the mouth of the Saginaw Bay. I told her I was trying to remember some things, and planned to visit the farm, too. Talking to her about Donny, about things he told her from his youth, could help. I wasn't looking for anything in particular, I said. "I mean, I don't know what I'm looking for exactly."

"Do you remember," Jan said, "that family gathering at Rita's place—in the mid-'seventies, I think—when we met?"

"I do," I said. "I guess that's the only time we have met."

"Your mother says you're always traveling."

"I've missed a lot of gatherings."

I hadn't planned to ask her any questions on the phone, but I heard myself say, "How did you and Donny meet?"

"He and my brother Richard were in the Navy together. Richard brought him home, to Bay City. That's where we were married—on October 27, 1956." Jan laughed. "It wasn't a Polish wedding, though. I'm Italian. Bacca."

In October of 1956 I was a freshman at Michigan State. Why didn't I attend their wedding? Surely I knew about it. I knew about girls and drinking beer and about Ezra Pound living in Italy and Hemingway fishing in northern Michigan—

"Two years later we had our Mary. She's a teacher now, would you believe it? I'm very proud of her. I'm proud of all my kids. Well, I might as well give you the whole list. There's Mary in 1958, Donny in 1960, Robert in 1962, Joey in 1963, and Frank in 1965."

After I spoke with Jan, I made two other calls to Michigan. The first was to Uncle Joe's son Jerome, who lives in Saginaw. I asked what he knew about Donny's last day. "He shot himself with a pistol," Jerome said.

"A pistol?"

"A little thing. A twenty-two."

I don't think I shouted *No*—meaning why would he choose a .22 for such an important job?—but I might have shouted the word because Jerome quietly suggested I call his sister-in-law Kim, who is a nurse. She could give me more information, he said, since she saw Donny soon after it happened.

Kim and Jerome's brother Steve live on a small piece of Grandpa's farm. But it's large enough, family word has it, for Steve to keep some animals and raise crops and produce with his owns hands everything he needs for his table. I had one good memory of this burly, bearded, self-reliant cousin: he was dancing a polka, round and round he went, now and then dropping down, almost sitting on the floor and kicking out his legs Russian style—an athletic, joyful performance. This was at the wedding of my brother Greg's son Grant, one of the few family gatherings I had been able to attend.

"They brought Donny into the Standish hospital, where I was working," Kim told me when I reached her. "He needed more help than we could give him, so he was taken to Saginaw. That's where he died." She heard that he lay in the Saginaw hospital and said nothing. I remembered the Model T on the farm that Donny tried to start, not wanting to drive it anywhere, just start the goddamn thing, make it roar. "Choke it! Choke it!" he yelled at me as I sat behind the wheel, while he, at the front of the car, furiously turned the crank. I think we got the engine to spit once or twice. I also recalled the log bridge over the creek where I tried to make the sound of *psia krew* come out right. I asked Kim if it was still there, and she said, "Log bridge?"

"On the farm," I said, "down the hill from the barn."

She wasn't sure she'd ever seen it, she said.

"In my memory it's quite large," I said. "You could drive a team of horses and a wagon over it."

"I'll ask Steve when he comes home," she said. She also said she was sorry she couldn't tell me more about Donny, but she wasn't really involved in his case.

"That's all right." I wasn't interested in the medical details anyway, and least of all in the legal detail. I guess I'd known all along what Donny had done.

Driving east on Interstate 80 across Illinois, south of Chicago you pass a huge hole in the earth, a rectangular, deep, gray limestone pit—a quarry whose produce has gone into road building—a quarry that seems just about played out . . . a mammoth hole that the diggers are moving away from, to start another elsewhere. What will this old one be used for? What *can* such a hole be used for? It looks big enough to bury the entire population of Illinois—and throw all the old TV sets gone fuzzy that people drag to the curb, hell, throw in all the junk from all the curbs in America! Every no-good, rusted out, busted, trussed-up piece of nothing you can no longer stand to be around—haul it all here over the stones pulled from this hole that are crushed and smoothed out to give you a nice ride, and toss it in. Then forget about it. . . .

In Pinconning, when I arrived, the sky was pure blue, and though I could not see it, I could smell the Saginaw Bay—that watery, dock-soaked, rowboat-and-weeds odor I always associate with perch on a string and buckets of silvery smelt and find rich in a tenuous, melancholy way: as the smell of a woods at dusk is rich, as the smell of old harness leather and the hickory handle of the hammer my father held are rich.

In the St. Agnes Cemetery Great Uncle Pete lay with his second wife, Katarzyna, and two of their children, Helen and John. Pete (1879–1947) died of old age, Katarzyna (1878–1936) of paralysis. The gorgeous Helen and handsome John (whom the French girl was crazy about) both died in 1937, at eighteen and twenty-two, the daughter from influenza, the son from dropsy. Most of these details are recorded in the St. Agnes parish books.

No doubt my grandfather traveled the short distance down from his farm to pay his respects and raise his glass. No doubt he drank whiskey with his brother at three of these funerals and then on 17 April 1947—Pete's funeral—he drank without him. Four days later he and Nelly had their forty-fifth wedding anniversary. Records. Dates. Names on paper and in stone and in the watery memories we carry . . . and they mean less and less, they become less and less as the various winds come and go, harsh and sweet, in their seasons.

Or they mean more, become much more, but how do we grasp it, that increase? that newness or strangeness? How do we recognize it, hold it?

During the Depression, the war, those years of too little and too much and of thinking hard about things that matter, my grandfather put seed in the earth and milked his cows; he watched the sky as farmers have always watched the sky, and believers, too, and those who fear, carry doubt; he thought of long-ago Ostrów, surely, and of youth, his brothers, a journey to America, his wife and children, of right directions and wrong. Surely he grieved over those loved ones, and those loved places, that were so changed nothing could bring them back the way they were; but surely he was consoled, too, thankful, for having been in their presence, and for being in their presence still in his mind and heart; and surely he was also angered, weakened, confused—perhaps at moments made mad—and perhaps those summers when I watched him gaze at the sky or bend his burning face to the water, perhaps those summers when I witnessed that impotent fist raised at the hail, that falling-on-his-knees embrace with the black bull that nothing it seemed could separate, perhaps in those seasons named sweet and harsh he was taken by all of it, them, continuance and silence, those two perfect blooms in the field beyond. . . .

Six miles up the road in Standish I ate lunch at Wheeler's, where my mother said she and my father had their first date. I had the special—Polish sausage and boiled cabbage. I faced a wall-sized sepia photo of Standish from the 1890s. As I looked at the frontier-like scene, at the unpaved main street, women in bonnets and children in overalls riding past store fronts in horse-drawn wagons, men up close on the board sidewalk in derbies and walrus mustaches staring at the camera—at me, eating lunch in Wheeler's—as I looked at these folks from a hundred years ago it struck me that some of them may have been related to me, were as much a part of Steve's story as Pete or Aunt Mary or my mother. Or myself. It was even possible that the man in the walrus mustache closest to the camera, a man whose fuzzy eyes seemed to want to avoid contact with mine, not recognize me, not recognize anyone connected to Steve Szostak—it was possible that he was the father of the man who fathered Donny. I looked at him until, crazily, hypnotically, I almost believed it.

I finished my lunch and smoked a cigarette. On another wall, in a frame, I saw the page for January of the 1937 calendar. Paying my bill, I asked the cashier—an elderly woman—if January 1937 was when Wheeler's opened for business, or if it went back to the 1890s. "Oh no, we opened in 'thirty-five—in the spring of 'thirty-five," she said.

That was the year my parents were married—in June. So they must have had their first date a couple of months before. But that can't be right, surely they courted longer than a couple of months. They met at a dance, my mother said. Then my father rode his motorcycle from West Branch to deliver notes to her mailbox—did that often—because Grandpa would not have a man bearing a German name on the farm. Since he was not allowed on the farm, my father had to win Steve's approval before he even met him—via good recommendations from my uncles, the gift of a hard-to-get tool, a bottle of rye. All this would take time. Then after Steve accepted my father and my mother's engagement was announced, they had to prepare for the elaborate High Mass wedding in St. Florian's with three priests, they had to butcher and make sausage, etc., for that three-day celebration in the apple orchard. No, no, my parents didn't have their first date in Wheeler's—not unless they managed to court and marry without ever having—in my mother's eyes—a real date, and *then* went to Wheeler's. Certainly that was possible during the Depression. Who had money for dates? Real dates. A wedding, however, was another matter if you had cloth to make a dress and pigs to slaughter and a swell place to dance.

Before leaving Wheeler's, I asked the cashier what the significance of January 1937 might be.

"Well," she said, "I don't really think there is any. Maybe," she laughed, "that's the closest they could come, you know."

"To the real date," I said.

"I suppose!"

Leaving Standish I passed the Arenac Lanes, where Donny had leaped up and down setting pins, and at the edge of town I passed the cemetery that held him still. Seven miles later I passed through Omer—"Michigan's Smallest City," a sign said. Other signs said "Erv's Upholstery," "Wildlife Creations—Taxidermy," "Deer Jerky." In the Omer cemetery Mary and her husband—a man they called Birdie—lay buried. Jan told me that. She also told me that Mary kept her marriage license on her bedroom wall. And Kim told me, "The first time I saw Aunt Mary—when Steve took me to met her and Birdie—she ran into the bedroom and hid."

Au Gres is six miles from Omer. I recorded this fact, among my other facts, in the Big Chief Tablet I had brought. I like these tablets. I was introduced to them years ago, at St. Joseph's School in West Branch, and I use them whenever I can get them. Nowadays they are hard to find. Perhaps because children are urged younger and younger toward the computer. On the cover there's a drawing of an Indian chief in his big bonnet of feathers, and underneath the chief are two lines to complete: "Property of ______" and "______ School." Simple enough. Then you go inside—

I had to laugh. Nothing big, more like a quick release of breath. I was remembering a question I had put to my dad: "What's the hardest thing in the world to do?" I had in mind an answer related to construction, for at the moment he was building a house for my dog. I was handing him the nails. He said, "Getting from here to there." I was puzzled. "To where?" I asked. "To wherever you're going," he said.

It seemed to me now as I made my way toward Au Gres that my father paused and looked at me as if he suddenly knew something—knew when we finished nailing together those boards we knelt among in our backyard, finished the job, that I would soon be starting to pack my bag, knot my tie, take his hand, and say I'll be seeing you.

It seemed to me now—if such a thought, about the swiftness of time, was contained in his look—that I left home before either of us would, or could, have predicted. Not after high school when I was expected to go, but those summers I went to the farm—when, delivered to my grandfather, I began to feel, and thrill to, a sense of separateness. We sat in the same orchard, stepped around the same cowflop, used the same bootjack, the same creek to wash off the same haydust, looked at the same sky, same stars, smelled the same dusk, and heard the same killdeer shrick its final evening song. But doing those things together did not make me feel close to him, connected to another, in a way I was used to. They made me feel closer to myself, to my own ears and eyes and the shadows and bright figures inside my head I wanted to follow.

Coming into Au Gres I remembered a Scotsman on the Isle of Skye riding his bike in the rain toward Portree. He must have been seventy years old, pumping his bike into town. I passed him in my rented car. At the Portree pub where I stopped, he came in and ordered a whiskey. He had a creased, weathered, shiny face and a bushy mustache. I bought him another whiskey. He thanked me for it by nodding once in my direction. We stood at the bar a few feet apart and drank our whiskies, saying nothing. He kept his cap on, his eyes in front of him; he might have been even older than I guessed. I liked that old man. I liked his rubber boots and baggy pants and creased shiny face and that small dark cap pulled down almost over his eyes. Driving into Au Gres past the bait shops and bars, I remembered how much I had enjoyed that day on Skye, the long walk in the Trotternish, in the green hills and fields above the sea, and then, at the end of it, drinking whiskey beside a silent old man who came to town on his bicycle and had no frivolous talk, no gab for a tourist, no need for anything outside himself it seemed except a little whiskey to warm his bones and a bar to rest his big-knuckled hands on. Leaving, he raised one of those hands in my direction, still not looking at me, and then went back to where he had come from.

Donny's widow lives in a neat little bungalow that formerly would have been described as log-cabin rustic. But she had the logs covered—outside with green siding, inside with plaster and flowered wallpaper. In the living room, on a whatnot next to the TV, she keeps several music boxes, including one she bought in Nashville that plays "The Tennessee Waltz." Also on the whatnot are wedding photos of her children. She is in some of them; Donny is in none. She has black hair and olive skin. Donny also had black hair and olive coloring.

We sat on the sofa. She handed me a small group of pictures. The one that held me was of Donny with his arm around Aunt Helen in her backyard in Detroit. He seems about twenty-five. He is wearing a suit and tie and a thin mustache. He looks like a sharpie, a gambler, a fast-talking comic in a strip joint, a guy who knows his way around. No—he looks like a young man trying his best to look good, be liked, a drummer-nephew who has just showed his aunt something she really doesn't need but okay, she'll buy it anyway, he's family, and they are both smiling, getting a kick out of standing there posing—the one all slicked up and the other who will accept him no matter how he looks because—

He was honorably discharged from the Navy, Jan said. They lived twelve years in Grand Rapids, where he worked for the Chesapeake and Ohio Railroad. They moved up to Bay City, where he took a job with Penn Central. After two years he was fired. "He was vice president of his union," she said, "and there was a disagreement. Donny took them out—on an unauthorized strike. Then we moved to Hickory Island."

The Navy—Grand Rapids—Bay City—Hickory Island. To an island?

"It's not a real island," Jan said. "It's the name of the street we lived on in Omer. Donny's mother and Birdie lived next door. Anyway, after getting fired he was out of work almost nine months. He finally found a job at Kraft Foods in Pinconning, in shipping. That's where he worked the last ten years or so of our marriage. . . ."

All these connections to water, I thought.

"You know," Jan said, "that he took his own life."

Her words fluttered like leaves around the photo I was holding. . . .

"It was October. We had been separated almost a year. I was living in Au Gres. He was living on Hickory Island with our sons Joey and Frank. Joey had left for work that morning, Frank for school. The house was empty. . . ." Mary, now a widow, Jan said, lived next door with her Pomeranian. The previous spring, Donny spent two weeks in Traverse City. A mood disorder, the doctors called it. He stayed in the same hospital Mary had been in all those years—and which he got her out of when he was in the Navy and brought her down to Pensacola where she watched officers' kids. Later she had to go back to Traverse City, and he got her out again.

Mary told Jan and Donny that she married a man named Harry Stark in Detroit after Donny was born, but she threw Stark out for fooling around on her. Donny told Jan he could remember living in Detroit as a small boy—a mounted cop gave him rides on his horse—but he didn't like the city, the noise, the confusion, and wanted to be on the farm with Grandpa. Mary told Jan that Donny's father was a man named Charles Schultz and Jan wondered to herself if the spelling of Donny's last name on his Baptismal Certificate—Schustak—was a combination of Schultz and Szostak. When Donny was in the Navy, Mary took him to meet Charles Schultz in New Orleans. Schultz was rich, Mary told Jan, and Schultz's mother was very good to Mary—but Schultz got mad at Mary and sent them away. Jan didn't know, not for sure, what all this meant to Donny. She did know that he loved Birdie—as everyone did—very much.

Jan stood up. She went to the whatnot and played "The Tennessee Waltz." Then she looked at me. I wanted to ask about Birdie. Why was he called that? Did he whistle like one? Did he have little tufts of downy hair over his ears? Could he cause sparrows to sit on his shoulders and peck seeds from his hands? He must have been a kind, gentle, happy man, yes? Jan said, "Donny was a good provider. We never had bill collectors. He believed if you borrowed a man's tool you returned it clean. He talked about wanting to farm again. . . ." But she finally had to move out. That mood disorder was too much. He was often afraid. He put notes in the neighbors' mailboxes telling them people were after him. He was up and down.

The woman who found him worked for Social Services; she had come to see Mary and then gone over to tell Donny his mother's Pomeranian needed grooming, she wasn't caring for it properly. Donny was in his pickup, it was early October, and the yellow hickory leaves were falling.

I remembered my dad's answer to the question about the hardest thing in the world to do. I also thought of Uncle Stanley's fierce eagle-like gaze in his Army picture, and that mammoth gray hole in the ground I passed, and the old Scotsman pedaling his bike in the rain.

At Least One Pure Disappearing Act

On the last Sunday of April, in Flint, I gave my talk at Dom Polski—the House of Poland. I wore a navy blue suit built for me by a Warsaw tailor. My mother sat up front next to her cousin Clara, whose parents, Mike and Helen Kapanowski, owned that saloon on the corner of Plumer and Junction long ago—where Steve Szostak went for his bucket of fresh beer. Aunt Rita and Uncle Tommy sat behind them. We were in the large social room. It was full. Just before I got started, my mother winked, holding up two crossed fingers wishing me luck.

I showed the audience my saber and told how I got it. Then I told about Blackie. In our season's opening game, playing first base, he made a nice catch of a high throw from the shortstop and the runner was out. Blackie was so pleased that he thrust a triumphant fist into the air and performed a one-man parade in front of the happy local crowd that took him and his euphoria into short right field. Meanwhile, a runner on second base, taking advantage of Blackie's celebration, ran to third and, seeing that Blackie was still full of himself, continued toward home. Blackie woke up just as the runner crossed the plate, and *then* he threw the ball to our catcher who, all this time, like the rest of us, had been shouting for it. Between innings I spoke to Blackie about this error. He hung his head—he would make amends. When he came up to bat, he hit a triple.

He stood on third base with his fist held high. From the coach's box across the diamond at first, I returned his salute. Then I signaled for him to take a lead. He could take a big one because both the pitcher and the third baseman were ignoring him. Instead, he continued to stand on the base, like a Polish prince who had just recaptured his rightful land—or a piece of it anyway—telling me (I could see the word issuing from his mouth, could almost hear above my own shouting its self-assured, completely-in-control tone), "Moment, moment." Blackie was at that moment a prince indeed—not a factory worker, not a twenty-two-year-old guy who still lived at home with his parents and grandmother in a cramped two-room Socialist flat because that was how it was in Poland then unless you had dollars, or joined the hated Milicja and right away got a nice apartment and a nice salary, or had some uncommon luck, which was mainly a myth. Yes, at that moment Blackie was in charge and he wanted to savor his territory, his victory, and again he thrust his fist to the heavens. Meantime, the pitcher delivered his pitch and the batter hit a routine grounder right to the third baseman. At *that* moment Blackie decided to conquer home plate. The third baseman, distracted, juggled the ball, then fired to his catcher. They got Blackie, who was very fast, by a step. Later, when I explained that had he taken even a dinky two-step lead he'd have been safe, Blackie hung his head like a man who had miserably failed everyone, including his parents and grandmother and the great Adam Mickiewicz, whose fiercely patriotic verses and plays gave the people hope when their country formally did not exist, and for whom Adam "Blackie" Ziółkowski was named.

Blackie and the other Sparks had fallen in love with this game they were learning, with its precision and grace, but in the beginning they too often played as if they carried sabers and were engaged in defending their honor, waging old and bitter battles against the Russians, Prussians, Austrians, Swedes, and Nazis—all those invaders who had stolen something irreplaceable from them. The Sparks were good athletes—former soccer players, javelin throwers, distance runners—and they wanted to be good at baseball, because of what it was, yes, but also because other things were involved. I was not interested in promoting metaphor—they already had that, deep in their bones and hearts; I only wanted to teach them such maneuvers as getting from here to there, from the batter's box to home.

I returned to the States and wrote that story. Then I sat with my mother in her backyard, splitting a beer, remembering things, and began this story—this search for my grandfather—starting with the summer I stayed in Flint and joined a baseball team instead of going to the farm, the summer I turned eleven and attended his funeral wearing a heavy blue suit. In many ways this story is a continuation of the first one. I understood that, imperfectly, all along. I understood it better when I came to the House of Poland in my Polish suit on the day after I drove to my grandfather's farm and kept going.

I took M-76 from Standish as we always had driving up from Flint, and looked for his long tree-lined driveway, his two-story yellow boxy house and apple orchard. I had just left Resurrection Cemetery in town where he and Nelly lay under their common stone, where Donny and Uncle Joe, close by, lay under their stones. Great Uncle Jake was there, too, off by himself but for once, at least, leading the way. He died on 16 June 1944, three years before Pete, five before Steve; there was a kind of numerical rhyme in their final dates: 6-16-44, 4-14-47, 8-18-49. When Nelly died, I remembered, I was in Mexico. When Uncle Joe died I was driving a restored 1946 Chevrolet from Iowa to Oregon, following old two-lanes over a northern route, taking my time, sleeping out at night under a wide sky. I heard about Joe's funeral, as I had heard about Grandma's, weeks after the fact. As for Donny's, I was in Iowa and my brother and sister had tried to call me, but I was writing a novel about a fine marriage falling apart and kept my phone unhooked almost all the time.

The funerals of Jake and Pete were events that passed me by—the fact that these men existed nearly passed me by. Why is that? Because they were simply two old guys from the Old Country who had done nothing except work hard and die, even though one was, by some, ordained a priest and the other given three wives to bury? If I had not poked around asking my questions, would I one day have heard such stories, perhaps at a funeral with distant relations, and raised my glass?

As for my grandfather's funeral, I rode up north for it with my parents wearing a wool suit that felt way too heavy for August, and therefore at one point during that long strange day when people came to view the body and say the communal rosary and stand around and talk, I went down to the creek and undressed and entered the water. I remember I pulled up big stones from the sandy bottom and threw them at boulders or if they were flat skipped them over the surface. I did that for quite a while pretending I was in a baseball game. I came out when I saw a bloodsucker on my foot. I rubbed it off with sand as Donny had taught me. Then I put my suit back on and returned up the hill. That it was my birthday was far from my thoughts. I was hungry. I hoped I didn't have any bloodsuckers on me where I couldn't see.

Now, driving on M-76 and looking for his farm, I saw nothing familiar, nothing at all, and then I came to Sterling. I couldn't understand it. I turned around and tried again. I drove all the way back to Standish. I passed only one farm on his side of the highway; it had a short driveway with a few saplings sticking up beside it, but there was no orchard, no old barn, no boxy house. There was a one-story modern house, a modern metal barn, and two or three blue metal silos.

Forty years after my grandfather died, I tried to find him. What does that mean? Does it mean finding his scarred reflection on the water—in the same place he had left it, among the minnows, among the wet boulders in the shallows where Donny had taught me to pitchfork suckers, among those sucking hoof prints Prince and Nelly made in the mud? Does it mean in late sunlight I can go back and find a frog occupying one of those hoof prints? a toad up the bank? and farther up, the black bull with its head held low even after he had let go of it?

In my mind I walk up the hill to his house and in the kitchen I watch him kneel beside the table. I listen to him murmur over those black beads, those sorrowful and joyful mysteries. I stay there in the lamp's honeyed glow, smelling the kerosene, smelling the sweet, sharp mix of whiskey and tobacco as he reads from his book about the remembered, the forgotten, the romantic, the hopeless, and the saved, and I read with him, a voyager too, a fellow immigrant, and time gathers, holding out things for me to see, clouds above the orchard, the figures there, the stories: gathers and goes about its business, round and round, and one of us is shouting *Gee!* and the other *Haw!*

Excited, I say, "Is *Heart of Darkness* the book Grandma put in your coffin?"

He only looks at me—from his formal wedding portrait, the one I received in the mail from Great Uncle Pete's son—

> Dear Gary,
>
> This is a picture of your grandfather and grandmother. I hope it will do.
>
> Stanley Szostak

—looks at me from 1902, ready for anything, including marriage, kids, hard work, success, America. He has a rose fixed to his coat, a cigar between his fingers, and beside him a young bride, a Polish-American girl who puts a hand on his arm and keeps it there for forty-seven years, and then just before Mr. Savage closes the lid, gives him a book about the passions and mysteries of the heart, a book about two foreigners making their separate ways in the jungle, one of whom is trying to understand the other.

POSTSCRIPT

After writing the above, I learned from St. Hedwig's that the lost Stella is buried in Holy Cross Cemetery. But Karol's final resting place is still unconfirmed. I am glad to know where she lies and just as glad not to know, for certain, where he lies. Let there be room in all families for at least one almost pure disappearing act. Nelly, no doubt, would claim he is in Heaven, which may be saying pretty much the same thing. I'm not about to argue with her. I'd rather applaud her for something she did not long before she died. She gave her youngest grandson, Steve Szostak—who lives on seven acres or so of modest farmland back in the woods beyond where a log bridge used to be—who thrives there by his own sweat and delights in it, and in dancing—she gave to him the original copy of her Marriage Certificate. Which is certainly no great thing in the larger world, where greatness is measured by grander deeds; but in the smaller world, where people work hard and die and leave only shards of themselves, moments, it seems to me just about perfect. Or close enough.

As for the modern house and those blue silos you can see from M-76, they belong to a dairy farmer named Jerry who is not related to any of us.

Covering Ground

"Are you back now?" Lizzie asks.

"I think so. I think it's done."

We have Henry and Ella on leashes and Margaret more or less between us, heading home from a refreshing loop in the timber. Just about a month ago Margaret turned four, and resists holding our hands. She likes to carry a stick, dawdle in puddles of melted snow, bend over an interesting stone or a snail shell she might want to fetch back.

"Guess what today is," Lizzie says.

"Saturday," I say.

"And?"

"Today is the day we covered some ground."

"You're not trying," she says.

"Margaret, what day is today?"

"A *good* day."

"Thank you."

The sun is easing toward the treetops. When it sets we will be in our backyard, watching, The Gospels in the distance turning, for several rich moments, an apricot color.

"It's Valentine's Day," I say.

"You peeked."

The truth is, I often have to stop and think about what day of the week it is. Yes, we own a clock, I tell our witty friends back east. Also indoor plumbing and long-playing records. That we do not have TV, that our phone has a rotary dial and no answering machine, strikes some folks as quaint. But we do have, among other refinements, the rare Calipso orchid come spring, and dogtoothed violets almost everywhere for a spell: bright yellow feminine petals—stars—blinking their news over the mountainside.

"Poppa, stop a minute. Listen."

We all stop. I hear them—the flock of wild turkeys. Then we see them making their way across a clearing up ahead; they look like turtles somehow in high heels, in no great hurry, though here and there one makes a fussy little spurt as if hissed at to get in formation. Some mornings they are lined up along the top rail of our corral fence gargling away like old dowagers on nice pensions; then they hop down, consorts heading for the open sea, flapping their jibs, know-it-all rednecks cheek by jowl with self-made millionaires who know it all too. I like having turkeys for neighbors; they are a solid source of information and they know when to go home.

"Some day," Margaret says, "I want to be smart as a tree."

I like having this kid around too. A few mornings ago she knocked on my studio door. "I have a question," she said. "What about when I was a baby?" I let her in. She was wearing two bathing suits—an orange one over a blue; her hands and cheeks were smeared green with watercolor; on her head a billed cap tilted back like my dad's carpenter's cap tilted back at the end of a hard day; and around her neck a string of paper pine trees, held together by Band-Aids, dangled down. "I'm trying to remember and I have to tell you," she said, "it's never easy."

In the photo album Lizzie made of our year in Slovakia, there are several pictures of the village of Čičmany that Margaret likes to study. The Čičmany folk houses bear carvings resembling hearts and rams' horns and hands raised in waving hello and tic-tac-toe boxes; the carvings are in logs that appear scorched from the long slow burn of time, a comforting lived-in color. The carvings themselves are highlighted with whitewash, applied often enough to keep them bright. No one in the village could tell us who made the carvings, though maybe, someone suggested, a certain very old woman might remember. In Lizzie's album the photos of these carvings are on the same page as the photos of the square we walked across in Medzilaborce—home of the Andy Warhol Museum—where following the revolution kids were given brushes and cans of white paint to do with as they pleased.

When George, Lizzie, and I entered the museum, a man named Jozef, from nearby Svidník, introduced himself. He worked in the museum, and he had the real story to tell us. He said that Mikova, a few kilometers away, was the true home of Andy's parents, Ondrej and Julia Varhola; and it was from Mikova that they fled to Pittsburgh after the First World War. (The brochure Jozef gave us said little Andy went with them and, in a manner of speaking, maybe he did.) But Mikova, such a tiny dot, where cows stood in the road, was hardly the place to build a museum, yes? Besides, Medzilaborce already had a building they could use, the old post office. It was falling down a little bit, but maybe with dollars from the Warhol Foundation in New York City they could fix it up! So now there was talk, letters back and forth, encouragement, delay, more talk, and more (the revolution had not happened yet, so things took time), and then, very quickly, the revolution arrived and soon an ultimatum from New York: act or forget everything. Oh boy. Jozef of Svidník sighed. By the way, he was a trained biologist, he told us, and also (this came out in a near-whisper, as if it was a near-miracle he was about to relate) he may have been related to Andy, because, you see, his mother's maiden name and Julia's maiden name were the same. Jozef paused so we could savor this.

Anyway, back to the nerve-wracking ultimatum. Time, time was hounding them, how could they fix up the old post office in time? Well, they couldn't. It was a mess, like a bomb, boom, had landed on the roof. So what to do? And then, like many small rockets, all eyes zoomed toward the huge, all-but-completed Culture Center that the Party had planned for *its* doings—big dinners, big displays, some drinking, you know—and, hey, they could take that building and all the money in the Party pot and make something nice for their Andy, yes? One funny thing, though, Jozef said: when they went to the money pot it was empty. He whistled, demonstrating how money can disappear. But they had the building anyway, and as we could see it was something—marble floors, high ceilings, good light, a big, perfect place. And at the dedication, Jozef said, everybody came, from everywhere.

We saw in this big place the actual baptismal garment, a white dress, that Julia took across the ocean to Pittsburgh and which the brothers Paul, John, and Andy all wore. We saw a postcard, of the Last Supper, which Julia sent to her sister back in Mikova after first improving it with a selection of colored pencils; we saw a photo of Andy, around ten, that, like the Last Supper card, was black and white before Mama put her hand to it; and then we saw several pictures done by brother Paul trying to get into the act. We saw a portrait done by Ultra Violet, of her and Andy, which she had donated and delivered in person a few months before. We saw a display of Andy's writing (he doesn't want a funeral, he says, he just wants to disappear), and beside this display a photo of Andy's conventional-looking grave in Pittsburgh showing that he got what he said he didn't want; and then we saw an announcement from Andy's nephew of his ordination into the priesthood; and then a wall the size of a moving van on which Andy's serigraph KRAVA (COW) was repeated over and over; and finally we left the museum feeling a little dizzy, as if we had been in a dozen places inexactly and too quickly, but walking across the square to which the children had given faces and bursting suns and waving hands we slowed down.

Lizzie, Margaret, and I have slowed down also: our hike, and now the afternoon sun, makes us drowsy. We come to a fallen fir knocked over by wind and age and composting nicely, rust-colored along its long length, and we sit there a while sharing orange slices. The dogs put their heads between their paws. Two winters back, I remember, in the Sawtooth Mountains up near Stanley, we found a hot springs at the end of the day. We were at 8,000 feet, though in the steamy pool we felt higher. When Margaret got in, she sang, "I'm naked! I'm naked!" and clung to herself as if the pink body under her slender arms might slip away. I did not want her to slip away, not ever, but I knew one day she would. I knew one day she would put on her snow boots and take up the trail in earnest—and I would call out I was happy for her, very happy, but sad, too, and hoped I would see her again. From the pool's moony wash she brought me her cupped hands. "Rock tea, Poppa, you like some?" Then she brought some to Lizzie. It was delicious, more delicious than anything we knew, than air itself, and we raised our cupped hands in the steam celebrating how far we had traveled together.

Living out here and having the whole day promotes such ceremony. But in my studio are certain documents that help clarify matters. I keep the Slovak residence card I was finally given as partial proof that, for a time anyway, I committed no criminal acts. I reckon it is not too unlike Great Uncle Jake's Certificate of Morality. I keep the saber the Poles gave me because how can I not keep it? Like them, I am capable of swinging a bat or running for home—or smuggling—as if my honor were at stake. I keep the phrase *Najväčšie akte* pinned up where I can see it because it contains one of those lessons, or warnings, easily nudged aside. The phrase, as Anna Grmela translated it, means, "who has the widest elbows." Soon after the Czech-Slovak divorce became final, she was telling me she had just taken a second job—in the Czech Republic—which would require her to spend twenty hours every week on the train, teaching three days in Prague, one in Prešov, back and forth like that, and why? Because she wanted to have a teaching position in Prague the following year when, she hoped, she and Josef would be living there permanently—and when Prague suddenly called and said now or maybe never, in a panic she said now, fearful that never would come and inhabit her like an empty stomach. That's when *Najväčšie akte* occurred to her. "Do you think I'm crazy?" she asked. "In America," I said, "you would be considered more or less normal."

My favorite Slovak phrase, which I don't need to pin up, is *za'hada*. Lower your voice a little, release that first syllable *za,* pause for an instant, then breathe out *hada* in two notes, thus *za—ha-da*. I went to see Bozka, the university's bookkeeper, about paying my rent. She found a piece of paper in her desk that said I owed 1,046 crowns. I said okay and a few days later returned with the money. This time she found a piece of paper that said I owed only 826 crowns. "I don't understand, Bozka." Then I bent close to her across the desk and whispered, "*Za'hada,*" and made a sweep of my arms to indicate that it—the mystery—surrounded us. She was a plump woman of forty or so with a permanent expression of sympathy in her large brown eyes. She glanced left and right as if someone might be close enough to hear us, though we were in her office with the door closed, and then she whispered back, "You are learning Slovak."

But I never did sit down—or even stand up—face to face with Franko, the former Party snitch. I wanted to meet him—and I let this be known—but my announcements must have scared him off. It was my own fault. I wanted a shoot-out, with witnesses, and he was too slippery, this man who, when the revolution arrived in Prešov, marched in the front ranks of the parade, the hammer and sickle pin on his lapel replaced by two new pins: an American flag and the Union Jack. Several students told me this. They also told me that he started up, quick-time, a private language school in town to teach English, assigning his university students to work in it, giving them grades of Excellent instead of salaries. He lived in a nice new house in Prešov where he hosted Western capitalists to discuss other ventures. Two students who cleaned his house—in exchange for top grades—let this be known. His doctoral dissertation, according to Igor, was a translation of *Death of a Salesman*—that is, a two-page summary of the play. I left notes for him with Monika inviting him to visit my class, to join me in lecturing on Arthur Miller; but his replies, to Monika, were always deep regrets: he would be out of town at those times. "A pity," she said he said, and rolled her eyes. "How is it possible," I said to her, "that he is never at the university anymore when I am here?" "Oh," she said, "it is very possible."

I suppose it hadn't helped matters when, at the beginning of that spring term, I created a little stir in room 90, which was where Monika said I would hold my Fourth Year American lit class. "Total," she said. I was happy. I knew room 90—it was big, full of light, and having it from one o'clock to four, three hours in a row for the lecture and the two seminars, we'd get a lot done. I went there. All my students, almost forty, were bunched up around the open door. They said the room was occupied. I went in. I found a professor settled at the desk facing seven students.

"Excuse me," I said, "I believe this is my room." I showed her the official assignment slip from Monika.

"Obviously a mistake," she said, and smiled. I knew that smile—everyone did—it meant: now that you have your information you may go.

I said, "You have seven students?"

"Maybe eight."

"I have almost forty."

She shrugged. Then she smiled again to indicate she was being very patient with me.

I found a ten-crown coin in my pocket. "Shall we flip for it? Do you understand chance?"

She laughed. "Yes, yes, I understand. But I'm afraid not, this is my room."

"No, no, it's our room, fifty-fifty. If we're both scheduled for it, we both use it."

Again she smiled—and slowly shook her head—as if to say really, enough is enough.

I shook my head back.

She said, "Well, I was here first."

My neck got hot. I went to the door to direct my students in. They didn't move. I reminded them of our fall semester wanderings; they were with me then, were they not, when we had to have class outside or in the hallways like refugees? Still they didn't move; they looked stunned. I went back to the professor. "Shall I send someone to find you a room?" she said. The patronizing smile was slipping off her face; her eyes, in fact, seemed tired. "Look," I said, "I'm not mad at you. I'm only frustrated." "Yes, it must be confusing for you," she said, "a guest, a foreigner. So"—she patted my hand—"I will go elsewhere." And she and her students packed up and left.

Relieved—also feeling guilty—I went out to fetch my students and they were gone. What to do? I returned to room 90 and sat down. In walked Igor, looking concerned. The students, he said, had just come to him and complained. I said they should complain—"we simply want a classroom."

"Yes, yes, there is that of course, but they complain you are not lecturing them."

"Right. I'm trying to give them complete stories, not summaries."

"Ah," Igor said, "there it is."

"There is what?"

"They are afraid they will not pass the exams."

"But they already have the questions, I gave them all out. Now we're looking at ways to respond."

"Ah," Igor said, "there it is."

I saw Eva poke her head in the doorway. "Are you all back?" I asked.

She nodded.

"Look," I said to Igor, "let's bring the students in and have a seminar on all this."

He hummed over my suggestion, looking at his shoes. While he was humming—and shaking his head doubtfully—I called to Eva, "Tell everyone to join us."

In they came, as if to a funeral. Most of them remained silent, but a few who rarely volunteered a word spoke up to say that my class was unlike anything they were used to. It worried them, they said. Eva, however, said maybe change was good. Two or three others timidly agreed. Then Vlado began to speak. Vlado, a poet, my most well-read student, said that he "and everybody else" wanted traditional lectures so they could learn how to become teachers. He said they wanted selections from those long works I was giving them. "Song of Myself," for example. Three or four lines—to get the general idea—was enough, he said. He said time was precious. Then there was silence.

I wanted to sit among them and raise my hand, say that going over "Song of Myself" line by line gives us the *poem*, the language, the country—shows us how and why Walt is so blooming American in the best sense. Ah me. Finally, I said, "Well, I can offer you a *Reader's Digest* condensed version of American literature," and Igor leaped to the balls of his feet, saying, "There it is! Exactly what you should do!"

It occurred to me, of course—more than once—that I was trying to sell the Slovaks something my fellow Americans were not all that eager to buy either. Although in the end we like a little verse to go with the candles and the coffin, owners' manuals and C-clamps are what we how-to people go for first. Recipes—of all kinds—formulas for where to squirt the oil, stick the tacks, stack the facts. "Is that a real poem," a youngster in Kansas once asked me, "or did you just make it up?"

Where am I?

When we go out walking, my daughter and I, just to go walking, and she finds a stone she never saw before, a flat yellow muddy stone with brown veins snaking through, and holds it close to her breast as she was held fresh from the womb, and says she must take it home for my birthday, to put a candle on it and blow until everyone is happy, and on the way sets it carefully down among the excited bees around her feet, because we've discovered some wild strawberries ready to pick and pick them, feeling those tiny surprising bursts in our mouths we never expected, and can't describe except by flapping our elbows, and then continue on up the mountain until the stone is settled beside my place at the table, waiting there like the freshest, most nourishing bread ever found on the land—I don't much care if all this began as a smooth, hot soup billions of years ago, or got cleverly whipped up by One with a fabulous sense of humor. I just don't want it to stop very soon.

Oshkosh the calico house cat we brought to Idaho comes to mind now and then, especially when Yah teh, who replaced her, studies the sky. Oshkosh took to studying the sky in a big way, so much so that after a spell on the mountain, getting to know it, there were nights when she refused to come in, preferring the moonlit deck, a rock in the orchard. Clearly she had converted to a wider view of things, and how could we blame her? One morning she was gone. We called, we searched, Lizzie even put an ad in the *Idaho County Free Press*. A forest ranger we spoke to said she had lost three cats within a year and could not bear trying to keep another one. Coyotes, cougars, hawks, owls—they were all too much.

Then something happened. *Bubo virginianus,* the Great Horned Owl—also called *cat owl*—began slamming into the house. I say that as if it were a common occurrence, but three times in a month seemed a lot, especially when we were eating lunch and suddenly there she was, beautifully spread out about a dozen feet from our tallest window, swooping down like

God's craziest angel. We were grateful and relieved, after the bang and fall, that she was able to fly—none too gracefully—but away she went to a big red fir at the edge of our yard, and settled her head, the finely barred pedestal of feathers holding it up, the famous eyes turned slitty, Oriental, as if nothing really had happened, my friends, and now it was time for a nap.

For as long as the owl sat there, Lizzie would move nowhere she couldn't keep an eye on the tree. She wouldn't whisper exactly, but if the radio was playing she quietly turned it off, and then picked up Margaret in case she might suddenly cry out. And then we waited, all three of us watching in a kind of belief I could never mock, Lizzie pressing her cheek to the baby's, saying, "See, honey?" And after a while, almost wistfully, "Well, we had fish again, didn't we?" And then when the owl finally leaped away down the valley, seeming on purpose to barely miss crashing into several aspen embracing autumn, "Oh! how she always needs to show off."

A year later, green-eyed Yah teh, a bone-thin kitten then, appeared in our barn. She lives there still, filled out, swift, and no doubt more savvy about the ground she walks on than the perhaps transubstantiated Oshkosh.

As for Henry and Ella, Lizzie found them in town, in a cardboard box near the entrance to Cash and Carry grocery. I was up the street, in Pioneer Park, catching Margaret who didn't want to stop jumping from the edge of the swimming pool. Lizzie appeared at the fence, saying we had to hurry up and come see.

"Is the parade starting?"

"They're perfect."

"Who are?"

"They were the last two!"

When Margaret and I got dressed, we saw Lizzie and some kids sitting in a circle under a tree. To their left, ladies in the food tent were shucking sweet corn, stirring pots, to their right a cluster of fiddlers was tuning up, and beyond them, in the middle of Main Street, girls wearing sequined shirts and Western hats flung batons in the air, practicing, waiting for the whistle. It was Fourth of July weekend; it was also our wedding anniversary. Could I think of a better present, Lizzie said, than two, fat, adorable, unexpected puppies?

I couldn't, especially after looking in their eyes as a parade honoring a significant event formed up in the background. It was, indeed, a memorable moment, and I prize it—just as I prize knowing the dogtoothed violets, and when they will start to show. I don't know how a dog's mouth got involved in their naming, but that doesn't matter. I know I can eat them if I don't eat too many, and come April when the snow is slipping in rivulets down my mountain, I know bear and deer will pause and enjoy them as I enjoy a truly fresh salad smelling of meadow and shaded wood; and I know in some ways we are all like dogs, or ought to be, in matters like faithfulness and sleep and nursing our young—and yet, knowing all this, I can't help thinking that these delicate, gold-colored wonders are much closer to a piano off in the wings bringing our daughters out in their toe shoes, that first bright performance at which we beam and beam until our hearts burst into flame. A tiny flame, yes? And lasting for only such a short time—the time it takes to compose ourselves, if we can, if we are that lucky.

Mid-March and the mountain's dirt trail I walk up, holding the pups' leads, is soupy. Flecks of isinglass glint at my feet, the sun cuts among slim tamarack, limbs snow-bowed for days slowly swing back—a jay jumps, rails on a stump and is gone. Under my shirt a letter from my mother says, "Look—for once you are not moving." It's true, in black and white the old Brownie snapshot shows Eddie Hill and me standing still.

I am tempted to stop and look at us again, at our mock-drunk grins and tipped sailor hats and the grapevines over our shoulders lush as cabbages, at the apple tree loaded with fruit—and beyond all that the figure of a man, way in the gray background, who must be my father just home from work. He must be wearing overalls, a pencil pushed under his cap, watching this moment more than forty years ago—caught there at the far corner where house, vines, tree, and he himself all seem to be falling into each other—caught there by my mother, who is trying to catch something closer.

But I don't take out her gift again, because suddenly I see the wild turkeys. Thirty—I count them—thirty wild turkeys mincing over Bailey's muddy pasture. This time they don't look like turtles in high heels but, all fluffed up, sharp as the hat Admiral Nelson turned just so during his heydays. The toms shake their wattles—bags of red flesh so freshly bright they might have been dipped in paint only seconds before I showed up. I crouch down level with Henry and Ella's pricked ears, hoping to see more: a battle, a dance—at the moment I can't remember what they do to determine the top cock.

Now, starting to complain about something—me? my dogs?—they send up their gargled hoots, screams of halfhearted outrage, and move away, closer and closer to the safe cover of a cedar copse bordering Bailey's pasture. I watch them go, philosophers, wags, coupon-clippers.

"Is this the life?" I ask Henry and Ella, feeling giddy, feeling the tension in their flanks to take off, pursue, and run until the running comes down to a dish of fresh water, a slow, comforting curl.

Two of us in that backyard I carry are gone, though if I reach under my shirt, which I can at any moment, we will all be there, still, or still enough, falling together near the end of summer, among summer's produce, faithfully practicing how to come out.

There is a picture that Lizzie took in Slovakia that never turned out exactly. Maybe we were all feeling too good and threw her off true when she was trying to set everything up. She'd placed the camera on a fence post, focused it, and was fiddling with the timer, warning us to get ready. It was a wedding picture—in an orchard, as a matter of fact—and the sun was rising on the second day of our celebrating Eva Zelena's marriage to a young man from Poprad. Not the essay writer whose words were displayed in the English department, but a man of equally strong feelings about apathy. He was a dairy farmer, blond-bearded and barrel-chested. He and Eva would live near the mountains that stood behind us. She had shown him *Walden* and "Song of Myself," he told me, and he liked them. "Listen," he said, and closing his blue eyes he recited, "'I think I can go and live with animals, they are so placid and self-contain'd.'" Eva, beaming, said, "Jarko is quite a husband already." He said, "I also like, in this Whitman, where he says animals do not cry about their station in life." "They do not *whine,*" Eva said. "*Ano, ano,*" he said, "a very good word, Eva. We must try never to do it. Wine to drink, yes, but not the other."

Lizzie was ready to start the timer on her camera and again told us to get ready. She ran to join us. Then Jarko remembered the part about the cow surpassing any statue, and said Whitman would have made an excellent dairy farmer. Eva began to tickle him. "You were so jealous of that man at first! Especially when I said *he* was my choice to marry on the exam, not Thoreau." "But I know why, of course," Jarko said, tickling her back. There were others at the wedding gathered around us, to also be in the picture, but none of us got in—except for somebody's hands reaching up as if to catch the sun coming over the mountains.